Coleman Curriculum for School Based Occupational Therapy

Thomas Coleman, OTR
Reaching Higher Therapy, LLC

WALDENHOUSE PUBLISHERS, INC.
WALDEN, TENNESSEE

Coleman Curriculum for School Based Occupational Therapy
Copyright ©2010 Thomas J. Coleman. All rights reserved.
ISBN 10: 1-935186-45-0
ISBN 13: 978-1-935186-45-8
Library of Congress Control Number: 2013917131
  "Introduces a curriculum for school based occupational
  therapy in the form of curricular strands, descriptive state-
  ments, and progress indicators. Intended for all grade levels
  of special education and primary levels of general education.
  -- Provided by Publisher
Printed in the United States of America.
Published by Waldenhouse Publishers, Inc.
100 Clegg Street, Signal Mountain, Tennessee, USA 37377
888-222-8228 www.waldenhouse.com

This book is dedicated to all of my family and friends who have supported my efforts, critiqued my work, and stood by me through this long, wonderful process.

To my boys, Kyle and Ian, I love you very much and both of you provide me with inspiration and joy every day.

To Etelvina, meu amor, your boundless encouragement and love have helped me to grow as an educator and author.

SCHOOL CURRICULUM OUTLINE

1) Introduction
2) Purpose of School Based OT
3) Vision
4) Tiers/levels of skill
   a. Average, typically general education
   b. Inclusion/low average, typically inclusion
   c. Below average, typically resource room
   d. Self Contained and/or severely handicapped
5) Plan
6) Benefits
7) Why non-special needs students would be in class
   when OT comes
8) Severely Handicapped Concerns
   a. Autistic Spectrum Disorder (ASD)
   b. Multiply Handicapped (MH)
   c. Medically Complex (MC)
9) Curriculum
   a. Description
   b. Outline of the Sections and strands

Appendix A. Alternate use section
   1. Focus guide
   2. Training
   3. Teaching aid
Appendix B. Research Study
Appendix C. Lesson Plans
Appendix D. Motor skill age equivalents for common
           academic tasks
Appendix E. Bibliography

INTRODUCTION

Coleman Curriculum for School Based Occupational Therapy has been born out of a need for reform and a belief that occupational therapy (OT) services can be delivered better to increase the benefit for the students, teachers, parents, and school districts. The special needs children and regular education children have curriculums for every subject except for therapy (occupational, physical, and speech). This fundamental need is finally addressed in this curriculum and guide (for occupational therapy only). Skills are discussed, examined, and brought to functional relevance for the benefit of everyone. Transparency and clear explanation of occupational therapy are addressed. Carryover of principles and activities to teachers and parents are of paramount importance to the success of the students.

Occupational therapy has increased in school districts every year, but the delivery of services has not changed at all. Students primarily receive pull-out therapy where they miss an academic subject (usually social studies, science, or elective) to receive therapy services. This puts the student at a disadvantage because now the student has to make up work or be instructed separately on the material missed. In my experiences, this method puts added strain on the teacher and student. Some students are so concerned with the work that they are missing that they do not completely focus in therapy. Some students become overwhelmed when they re-enter the classroom due to the make-up work. Teachers and parents are also affected because in this model the time with the student is paramount so little time is allotted for teacher or parent instruction.

Other service models for OT include push-in and consultation. Push-in equates to the therapist sitting in the classroom with the student to help the student in whatever manner the IEP states (handwriting, sensory, attention to task, etc.). Push-in therapy can be challenging for everyone involved because the teacher has added pressure to ensure that the lesson plans are current so that the therapist is working with the child on an academic area relevant to the skills being worked on in OT per the IEP. The student might feel self conscious because the student may be the only student who receives OT. The therapist is limited to what the teacher is instructing in class and do to the speed or nature of the lesson plan may not have time reinforce or go over skills do to lack of time. Consultation is typically 1 time per month or several times during the year to ensure that the student maintains skills acquired in OT and continues to apply them in the academic setting.

Skills are also broken down into tiers or levels as the primary tool for occupational therapy. This shift in focus will allow the parents and district to focus on what skills are deficient instead of what classification the child has. As a therapist, I can teach a student how to hold a pencil, but I can't teach a student not to be disorder "x". Instructing to a label does not benefit the person with the disorder, but addressing their skills can increase self esteem, skill mastery, and compliance.

As the focus shifts from classification to skill sets, carry-over will increase as well. The teachers and parents want to help their children, but in the current system they don't always know how. The clarification and transparency of what OT can do and should do for their children has never materialized in the pull-out model. Curriculum means the guide of what is taught. Parents and teachers need to know the guide to what OT teaches their children so that they can use it and help their children.

The research study completed using this curriculum demonstrated a positive effect in multiple ways in the preschool where the study was completed. Pre and post testing verified that the students as a whole improved slightly, but the best part of the study showed that two students made big improvements. As a therapist or teacher, anytime one of our students grows in a substantial way, there is a great sense of pride and joy. That pride and joy in my students is how I feel about this curriculum. It is my passion and my belief.

Another benefit from the research study became the increased knowledge of the teacher. The weekly lesson plans were clear and have a section marked collaboration so that the teacher knew exactly what skills were the focus for that 30 minute classroom run activity. The teacher stayed in class for every group so that she could work hands-on to see how occupational therapy addresses skill acquisition and that gives her the knowledge to carry through with those principles during class. The research study lasted for 12 weeks and proved a positive endeavor for all involved. Hopefully, a longer research study with more participants can be performed to cement this curriculum as a valuable tool for educational systems.

Please use the curriculum and knowledge in these pages to enhance the delivery and efficacy of occupational therapy services for everyone. It has been my extremely joyful for me to work, research, and study ways to make my profession better for the entire educational community.

Purpose of School Based OT

To determine the purpose of school based OT, we need to first discuss what OT is and what an OT does in a school system. OT is deemed a related service as it assists the students in meeting their academic needs at the most independent level possible. The OT performs functions for the students, parents, and teachers. The OT reports directly to the Special Education Coordinator or to a senior therapist depending on the district size and administrative hierarchy.

The OT helps the student to reach their maximum potential by teaching the student the skills necessary to complete academic work at their level. This can include fine motor, perceptual, visual motor, gross motor, and sensory skills. OT's help students improve these skills so that they can perform activities like handwriting, cutting, shoe tying, etc. These activities are important because they are part of the daily school routine that students can struggle with. Improvement of skills can help students to perform along with their peers at an appropriate pace.

The OT helps the teachers by teaching and training them on activities that promote skill attainment. For example, pinching activities can be used to help a student hold a pencil more appropriately. These interactions with the teachers are important for carryover because if the students perform the activities the proper way everyday then those skills are going to become mastered and permanent. In the current system, carryover is difficult because teachers are not in the pull-out sessions to see what is being done, time is not allotted weekly for teacher training, and the teachers do not have a singular reference for school based therapy.

The OT helps the parents by sending homework or correspondence. The parents have the opportunity to carryover activities at home. These activities can be as simple has holding the pencil differently or complex such as visual motor worksheets.

The students thrive when the parents are actively involved in carrying over skills learned in the school setting whether it be OT or math or reading.

The OT helps to serve the district and community by providing therapy services in a responsible way. The most challenging aspects about the current system are structure and time. The therapist is a licensed medical professional in an educational setting so there is rarely an OT as a supervisor or leader in the administration. The time constraints exist because in pull-out therapy your schedule has to have children that are being seen in your time slots to be productive. You cannot have open slots in your schedule in case things like meetings or conferences happen, but when they do you have to adjust your schedule accordingly. It is the most challenging aspect of OT in the educational setting. This curriculum and program address these and the preceding concerns.

The Vision

Coleman Curriculum for School Based Occupational Therapy reflects the belief that all special needs children can benefit greatly from a new education model approach concerning how occupational therapy is delivered in the school setting. The model focuses on skills rather than disabilities, quality of OT services rather than quantity of OT services, and carryover and shared knowledge with all educators. The transparency and solidity of a singular curriculum addressing students by skill level with the expectation of carryover from other professionals and parents does nothing but make OT work harder than ever for the student. This model is exciting because it truly puts the student first.

The need for the foundations of learning has increased as society has changed because we are a results based society. Students have access to technology that lets them bypass the foundation and go straight to the result. The system measures everything on testing, not on interaction and creativity. Other cultures have creativity classes to teach students to think outside the box so that they can problem solve later in life. Think about it, the best doctor I ever had listened to me and figured out my specific problem. The worst doctor I ever had read films and pushed surgery because that is what the book tells you to do. Testing at such a young age tells the student that results matter more than the process. That has never and will never be true because learning is lifelong and principles last, not facts. Trial and error bring about excitement and exploration more than any test can. These deficiencies in these primary skills manifest themselves later as compensatory methods and frustration as children are burdened with increased educational demands every school year. The lack of focus on the skills that are going to make tasks such as handwriting, note taking, and arts and crafts easier has put the special needs student at a greater disadvantage than in previous years.

The Vision for *Coleman Curriculum for School Based Occupational Therapy* is influenced by the understandings of the shortfalls of the current system and the belief that through reform the system can be made better. The therapist belongs in the classroom teaching the students and teachers skills to make academic life easier and more rewarding. OT is not meant to be relegated to a closet where you work with a child in private. The skills need to be addressed in the students environment with the people the student interacts with everyday to make the skills last. The teachers, parents, and districts need to know exactly what the therapist does to increase the foundations for the academic skills of the student.

The current system for delivering occupational therapy creates tension and unease. Tension is not a positive learning environment. Students know that when they are pulled out that they have to make up the work which creates stress. The teachers know that as well and become stressed. The therapist becomes stressed because they know that the student needs the help to catch up to his peers, but might be too taxed to make up the work in an appropriate amount of time. Everyone involved feels the stress and is affected by it. The vision of this curriculum and plan is to reduce the stress and make the learning environment more positive.

The current system also creates stress in another way by making OT an object or a commodity to be given out to the students. This perception creates tension at IEP meetings and has actually resulted in lawsuits. Parents, teachers, districts, therapists, and students all have their own perceptions and reasons for wanting or not wanting OT. The therapist reasoning is typically the most objective and most rational because as therapists we use objective measurements and observations to justify therapeutic services. The parents and teachers have more subjective and emotional input that can be based on their own perceptions. They view OT as an object that they can not let go of, that if it is not in their child's IEP the child is losing something. They can perceive that since their child is special needs they are entitled to OT and every other service available because of their child's classification. They can get stuck letting their decisions be based on fear instead of truth.

This vision brings truth to OT in school systems. The truth is that skills are the reason that students require OT, that skills know no classification or disability label. The truth takes that fear out of the equation. The vision further takes the fear out of the equation by having OT be a weekly 30 minute class where special needs student can get OT skill training from Pre-K to third grade. The vision is that the students, teachers, and parents get a singular curriculum that they know and trust to work with for Pre-K to third grade. OT is no longer an object, it is now a class focused on teaching the medical knowledge applied to academic tasks to increase skill sets which leads to student independence. It is a class focused on transparency and sharing of knowledge. It is for the betterment of everyone involved. The plan and subsequent chapters will explain the specifics in more detail, but to appreciate the plan you need to know the vision. Just as the student needs to acquire the skills to complete the tasks, the educator needs to know why they are doing something before they do it.

Tiers/levels of skills

The new thinking of levels of skill over just classification will allow the therapist to influence the school in an entirely new and profound way. The most basic approach to determining skill level is to pair it with classroom settings as the school has already grouped students by grade and academic level. There is the general education level where most students are placed. There are also three types of classroom options available in most public schools for special needs students which goes from (least to most restrictive) inclusion to resource room for language arts and math, and self-contained. This typically correlates into similar therapeutic and support needs.

Before fully discussing the tiers, the sections of the curriculum must be addressed. The curriculum is divided into two sections, Section 1 and 2. Section 1 addresses elementary school level needs for general education and special education students. Section 2 relates to vocational skills for special education middle school and high school students. This section is especially important to program like a structured learning experience and a self contained classroom where vocational gains might be the primary concern over collegiate work.

So starting with Section 1, the general education classroom level is included in this curriculum for Pre-K and Kindergarten. This is due to the fact that these years are crucial years for fine motor, visual motor, and sensorimotor development. The curriculum can be beneficial to this age group as evidenced by the research study completed using this curriculum in a 4 year old preschool setting. The research demonstrated a benefit for the students as well as the teacher. The use of a curriculum helps the students and staff carryover skill acquisition as instructed by the occupational therapist. Curriculum is the how to and what is to be taught. By providing teachers at all levels information on how and what occupational therapy covers in a school setting can lead to further collaboration and effectiveness.

The inclusion class is a mix of regular education students with some special education students. These classes typically have an in-class support teacher to help the special needs students keep pace with the other students. These students have an established skill set as they are performing grade level material with their peers with support. At this level, most of the students need that little extra to keep up with their peers. It could be a better pencil grip to increase handwriting neatness, visual/perceptual strategies for copying/note-taking, or postural strengthening exercises to increase attention. This would be extremely beneficial to teachers to have a reference for this knowledge shared to increase carryover. The curriculum would also allow the therapist to have a directing role when in the classroom instead of passively following the teacher.

The resource room class is typically comprised of students who require extra time and help with language arts and math. These students could have more difficulty with cognition, memory, problem solving, motor coordination, or other problems. These students are typically with their peers for science, specials, and social studies. These students can also do very well and progress to inclusion or the general education setting. The students at this level can be so varied in motor skills that a curriculum would be extra beneficial for parents and teachers to know what the expected normative values are for skills such as pencil grasp. During my years as an OT, this group of students has always been the most varied and would benefit greatly from a uniform curriculum.

The self contained classroom is typically for children who require very small group instruction due to a host of difficulties. These students typically have teacher's aides in the room for the class and some students may have a one-to-one aide due to behavior, physical, or cognitive issues. These students are in the same classes together for the entire day. They are pulled out for related services.

Due to the challenges faced in this population, the curriculum needs to address this tier level in a different way. The progress indicators need to be pushed back to allow extra time for these students to reach those goals. For example, the initial progress indicator for Section 1 of the curriculum is Kindergarten. This may not be appropriate for these students so the initial cumulative progress indicator would be third grade and the third grade cumulative progress indicator would be moved to 5th grade. This correlates to the elementary level of education and is usually completed in one school. This distinction is important because the purpose of school based OT is to help the students achieve functional independence in their academic setting. If a self contained student continues to complete basic academic work in grades 3, 4 or 5 then that student should have the OT curriculum correlate to those tasks that support the basic academic work such as handwriting, cutting, and self help skills.

The purpose of the tier system is to help set parameters and expectations for student achievement. School based occupational therapy does not have a designated end or beginning. The process of obtaining school based OT relies on referrals and evaluations. When we adopt a tier system with a set curriculum, parents, teachers, and therapists can utilize a guide to treatment expectations in not only terms of length of therapy services, but skills to be achieved. Referrals and evaluations should not be eliminated because they are valuable tools to ensure that students who might require therapy are not missed. The following chapter outlines the plan on how the curriculum, referrals, and evaluations should be utilized to most effectively deliver school based occupational therapy services.

The Plan

The pre-school and elementary levels are where the OT has the most impact and that is where the plan begins. The current model requires many evaluations to determine eligibility and to maintain eligibility. By adopting the tier system and beginning in Pre-K or Kindergarten, most students can be screened and the rest evaluated. Each Pre-K or Kindergarten classroom could utilize an OT weekly integrative session to work on motor skills. The therapist can make lesson plans, continually evaluate skill levels, and train the teachers on motor skill development. This can be in general education or special education classrooms. As stated earlier, the age levels of three through 5 are prime years for motor development. By acknowledging these facts and being proactive the students can receive highly skilled intervention at its most appropriate time. The current system of waiting for a problem to develop and then addressing it is illogical. For example, between the ages of 5.5 and 6 years it is developmentally appropriate for children to develop a mature pencil grasp. Instead of allowing the student to compensate, develop a poor grip, and wait for an evaluation referral years later, why not prevent such struggles? There are basic components of a pencil grasp that allow for more precise and controlled handwriting. These develop in Kindergarten so it makes sense for an expert on motor development to tackle this important issue.

If proactive style classroom interventions are not adopted, then the special education tiers of inclusion and resource room would be screened to determine a baseline of skills for a group to be run in those special education classes. The severely handicapped would be evaluated. This distinction is important because the severely handicapped have quality of life issues that are much more specific than educational goals only. Unfortunately, some students have significant medical issues where therapy influences their quality of life more than their education. Once the child is screened or evaluated then the therapist running the weekly class would know their baselines.

The plan is further divided by grade level as well. There are 4 basic grade levels in the public school system: Pre-K, elementary, middle, and high school. Elementary school is further divided into K-3 and 4-5 as related to the importance and relationship of milestone development to educational demands and performance. This distinction and value placed on the developmental years follows scientific research that early childhood therapeutic interventions show increased and substantial long term results. These specific interventions include, but are not limited to, visual motor, motor planning, fine motor, sensory motor, postural control, attention to task, and social skills development. Occupational therapists specialize in these interventions which are critical for children to succeed in an educational setting. This knowledge also makes it the OT's responsibility to share and train teachers about these therapeutic interventions so that carryover is achieved. For these reasons, that is why the curriculum goes to grade 3. The curriculum is based on developmental milestones and the research that students benefit greatly from early therapeutic intervention.

The integrative/curriculum model does not suggest classroom instruction beyond third grade because all developmental milestones should be reached by this point except for the severely handicapped. These students require an evaluation after third grade to determine what their needs currently are and what therapeutic interventions would be necessary to maintain or improve their quality of life. This is important because as a caring and humane society the severely handicapped deserve to have a dignified quality of life. In this area, societal and education concerns overlap because the therapist may focus more on positioning and stretching than letters and numbers because the teachers can focus on that. The therapists are trained with the background medical knowledge to provide that type of support to the severely handicapped student.

The two other tiers would get an exit screening, but not an evaluation. An evaluation would be based solely on individual need for continued therapeutic services. This is important because the student should have attained the skills necessary to complete academic tasks with their peers beyond third grade. The key is the skills, not the exact results. One of the major challenges in school based occupational therapy is explaining the difference between penmanship and fine motor deficiency that causes poor handwriting. It is very typical for an educator or parent to say that they do not want therapy discontinued because the student's handwriting is messy. The key question is, "Can the student write neatly properly forming the letters and numbers?" A lot of times the answer is yes, but the student "rushes" or is "not focused" when writing. This instance is penmanship and occupational therapy is not functionally warranted for penmanship. This is the hardest concept for parents and educators to grasp because handwriting has a personality and psychological component that is not changed through OT.

Another thought on the changeover to 4th grade and the discontinuation of integrative OT services is the accumulation effect. At this point, if the student has had weekly integrative OT since Pre-K (3 yr. old class) and the school year is 40 weeks long then the student will have had 240 OT sessions by the end of 3rd grade. This translates into 120 hours of instructional time for the student and teachers. It is irresponsible for the therapist, teachers, parents, and districts to not be accountable for this extensive amount of time in some way. This model recommends an ending to be pre-determined based on milestone and academic skill development.

For middle and high school special needs students, the focus of OT should shift to vocational skill completion as handwriting interventions at this point are not as beneficial. Direct OT intervention is also uncommon at this point for most students, except the severely handicapped and some self contained students. Section 2 of the curriculum has three strands that relate to vocational skills. These strands do not address specific tasks of specific jobs. The New Jersey Core Curriculum Standards address standards related to vocation and are covered by educators. The difference in vocational strands in the OT curriculum and the New Jersey Core Curriculum standards lies in the distinction of skills. There are academic, universal, and safety skills that are essential to workers that might not be as easily attained for the special needs population. For example, following directions is requirement for almost every job so it is appropriate to address that skill in the realm of OT rather than the OT focusing on directions for a specific task that only one or no student is completing in school.

The last aspect of the plan is the district's choice for a primary intervention in regards to behavior interventions in regards to OT. There are two primary interventions used in OT to improve behavior, behavior intervention (Applied Behavior Analysis-ABA based) and sensory integration theory. Unfortunately, these interventions are contra-indicated for each other when used equally. One needs to be primary and the other needs to be secondary. The best example of the contra-indication for these strategies is a special needs student who self stimulates by flapping his/her hands. The behavior approach would make the student stop the behavior for a certain amount of time before receiving a reward for appropriate behavior. The sensory integration approach would be to give the student deep pressure input or a fidget toy to help the student to calm down. If on Wednesday, the student flaps his/her hands and gets penalized by having to wait for a reward for appropriate behavior then on Thursday flaps his/her hands and gets a fidget toy (reward as seen by the student) as soon as he flaps his hands, then how can he/she consistently understand what is expected from him. It is unfair to the student to confuse rewards and punishment and it reduces the effectiveness of both strategies when used inappropriately. The key is to make one primary and one secondary. The best example of this delineation of importance is to make behavior primary and sensory integration secondary by scheduling the sensory time in each day. If the sensory time is scheduled then it is not deemed a reward or punishment, but rather a regular part of the day or week. The distinction of primary versus secondary would be determined by the district. The first two strands address attention to task with OT.1 addressing it with SI as the primary and strand OT.2 addressing it with behavior as the primary tool.

Benefits

The curriculum benefits students, teachers, parents, and districts on many levels. The uniform or central benefit to all parties involved is the transparency of OT as a related service in education. The knowledge and importance of OT is now visible to everyone involved so that there is a clear understanding of when OT's role is valid and when it is invalid. When OT is warranted and when it is not warranted. The benefit of a new perception allows the truth to be seen in what OT can and should do for the special needs population in an educational setting.

The direct benefits for students include teacher carryover to increase permanence of skills, less class time and class work missed, and a new focus on skills that will translate into future academic activities. The student will achieve permanence of new skills faster when they are continually reinforced in the classroom by teachers and teacher's aides. The reduction of stress as less work is needed to be made up will be extremely beneficial to the student. Many times students are pulled out and do not want to go because they are worried about work that must be made up.

The direct benefits for teachers include understanding and increased training on OT, ease of scheduling, and less make-up work. The teacher can become self confident in applying the skills taught by the OT because the teacher is in class with the OT as the OT completes the weekly lesson. The ease of scheduling is of paramount importance as the teacher does not have to remember who is pulled out when and where for what. Many teachers get frustrated that the student has to miss academic subjects like science and social studies for OT even though the teachers agree that the service is beneficial. This reduces or can altogether eliminate the need for make-up work in regards to a student missing class for OT because the OT is now a scheduled class.

The direct benefit for parents includes a clear understanding of what an OT does, less stress at IEP meetings in regard to procurement/discharge of OT services, and knowing when and where their child receives OT. In many school districts, space is an issue so OT has been done on stages, in hallways, and in gyms. Therapists are forced to carry equipment to and from school everyday because there are no spaces for them. Many parents are not happy that their children have to have OT in these conditions, but with this curriculum the student would have OT in his/her environment, the classroom. The reduction of stress for parents at IEP meetings is also important because so much good energy can be wasted on worrying before the meeting and having your guard up during the meeting over related services. As talked about earlier, the curriculum allows the CST to focus on the skills of the child rather than seeing OT as a commodity that you do or don't have. The idea of a set OT program will ease parent's concerns and worries.

The direct benefit for the school districts are reduction of costs, increased transparency from an outside vendor, and increased principles. The reduction of costs can be up to 50 percent for OT depending on the size and scope of the district. This occurs because now the students are in a group instead of individual treatments. To bring back the 120 instructional hours example, if that number is per group instead of per child then the costs go way down. For example, if I service 20 kids in 5 classes individually for 30 minutes per week in a pull-out setting then that is 10 hours instructional time (20 sessions X .5 hours/session = 10 hours). If I have the integrative OT curriculum in those 5 classes then with 30 minute prep, 2.5 hours of instructional time with the kids (5 classes X .5 hours/class = 2.5 hours), and 60 minutes of instructional time with the teachers then the billable time for the district would be 4 hours, a 60% percent reduction in cost. Not only is there reduction in cost, but notice the 60 minutes per week for teacher training. The old method of pull-out did not allot for any teacher training let alone 60 minutes per week. Everyone in the district benefits due to the increased quality of OT as a related service and a subsequent reduction in costs.

Why Non-Special Needs Students Would be in Class When OT Comes

Every student can benefit from refinement of skills, especially in the primary grades where skill building is essential for future academic success. For example, the mature grasp that most adults used is not developed until age 6, which is equivalent to first grade. This is a universal skill that regular and special education students require and it is one of the areas of expertise for an OT due to our training in anatomy, neuromuscular development, and hand skills. This is also an important change in perception as the stigma of special education is slowly eroding. The students today are expected to do more in less time and need educators to focus again on the skills that they will need to succeed instead of teaching for the test.

The secondary benefit to instructing OT with regular education students in the room is that those students can now model and demonstrate for their peers. In this age of specialization, students do not get the chance to interact with their peers as often. The self-esteem and confidence that students receive from helping other students is invaluable. The act of teaching increases the appreciation for learning which is so valuable as students progress through the public education system. Learning is a lifelong process and the more students appreciate learning, the better they will do in school.

Finally, the last benefit for students is to be proactive to see problems before they happen by reducing compensatory strategies. Often times students will compensate to achieve desired results because education has become results based. The student that writes their name well at age 4 with a poor pencil grasp and poor letter formation will have a greater chance of having difficulty taking notes and keeping up with the class as the work load increases because those poor habits were never corrected. The early results that mask deficiencies are detrimental to the student in the long run.

Severely Handicapped /Self Contained Student Concerns

The severely handicapped student requires increased medical, emotional, social, therapeutic, and academic support. School districts do a very good job of meeting these needs or send the student to a private school that can fulfill those needs. School districts understand that there is a societal responsibility to educate and care for these children. Severely handicapped students receive educational support until the age of 21. For many of these students, work or college post graduation is very challenging due to either physical, mental, cognitive, social, or a combination of one or several of these disabilities. Therapeutic concerns for these students include addressing a combination of quality of life and academic needs. There are three subtypes to the severely handicapped, which are as follows: Autistic Spectrum Disorder (ASD), Multiply Handicapped (MH), and Medically Complex (MC). Each subtype shares many common ailments, but each subtype also has specific concerns that affect the therapy model.

ASD students are perhaps the most complex students for a myriad of reasons. Firstly, no one truly understands the cause for the disease. Scientists are identifying genes that could be responsible for ASD spectrum disorders, but no one has a definite answer yet. This can be maddening for some parents because how can you fix a problem if you don't know how or why it has occurred. Secondly, ASD spectrum disorders increase the likelihood of an accompanying mental disorder diagnosis by tenfold. Any secondary diagnosis can exacerbate the ASD spectrum symptoms making it more difficult for these students to function in school. Thirdly, there is not one single intervention that works for every child. Parents have used Applied Behavior Analysis (ABA), Sensory Integration (SI), Therapeutic Listening Program (TLP), nutritional supplements, hippotherapy, and more to help their children. Some of these interventions work well for one child, but do not work well at all for the next child. The lack of knowledge of the disease and the inverse or plethora of interventions to treat the disease can confuse and upset parents, school districts, and therapists.

MH students are typically students who have neuromuscular diseases accompanied by cognitive, emotional, or mental disorders. The focus for them continues to be quality of life because the things that we do easily everyday can be very challenging for them. Sitting in a chair, standing up, or raising an arm might be physically challenging or beyond their scope of performance. Wheelchairs, specialized chairs, standing tables, and splints/braces are commonly found in these classrooms. Therapeutically, these students typically require more hands on work of positioning in their wheelchair or stretching to reduce or maintain muscle tone. There is no specific curriculum section for these students because the basic skills that they need are more medically based and therefore more individualized in nature. Some students unfortunately may be in a wheelchair for the rest of their lives or always need braces to walk so they would not fit into a curriculum. To reduce costs, therapist can train teachers and therapy assistants to complete more of the hands-on work required for these students as the therapy switches from skilled services to maintenance services. The best example to show the difference between a skilled service and a non skilled service would be the therapist evaluating the child and saying he has these deficiencies that require this stretching and splinting schedule. The therapist would then train a teacher or aide on the schedule. Once trained, the teacher or aide can follow the schedule. Following a schedule is not a skilled service.

MC students are typically students who are severely impacted by congenital medical deficits. These students can be impacted by rare genetic diseases or suffer from a traumatic injury. These students can require special medical equipment such as feeding tubes or prosthetic devices. They can also require the services of a Registered Nurse (RN) for maintenance or application of such devices. The therapist has to be cognizant of these co-morbidities to effectively assist the student. The focus for therapy is a combination of quality of life, medical necessity, and academics. The therapist can also act as a liaison to the teacher for explanation of medical jargon.

Overall, the severely handicapped require quality of life along with or more than academics. The responsibility of the school system is twofold as districts must cope with the demands of these students on every level. Therapeutically, these students require increased postural, positioning, adaptive equipment, and hands-on techniques that are not appropriate for a higher functioning curriculum. These students require more teacher and staff education to continue with the skilled services that the therapist uses to determine deficiencies and needs. Therapy assistants are also valuable to this population to continue with the skilled programs set-up by the therapist.

The Curriculum

The body of the curriculum is divided into 2 distinct sections. Section 1 includes 13 educationally relevant occupationally therapy standards for the general education and special education students in the elementary level. Section 2 has 3 strands and is designed for the middle and high school levels. In Section 1, each strand has a number of identified strands with two levels for assessment, Kindergarten and third grade. These two grades are developmentally significant for the purpose of this curriculum. In Kindergarten, the student takes the pre-writing and pre-academic skills learned in Pre-K to begin an increased academic workload. It is important for the pre-academic skills necessary for higher grades be addressed here. Third grade is important because at this point the shift has dramatically swung to almost all academics and limited pre-academic skills. This is extremely relevant because OT focuses on skill attainment, not academics; therefore it would behoove the occupational therapist and educational staff to utilize OT when it is most beneficial and make that a primary focus.

The curricular strands focus on specific components such as fine motor skills and skill components related to an academic area such as math. Most people do not associate math with OT, but if you look at the basic skills of mathematics, than OT is appropriate. Occupational therapists can focus on sense of quantity, math language, and problem solving skills. The school based OT would not make a lesson plan entirely based on mathematics, but could include it in the lesson plan. A great example of this is the research study completed on this curriculum. During lesson plan 6, Standard OT.10 was utilized to address the mathematical concept of sense of quantity along with Standard OT.1 (cause and effect), and Standard OT.12 (gross motor, specifically shoulder girdle strength). This can be further correlated to the teacher lesson plans to make the OT time in class a further reinforce for skills learned instead of pulling a child out of class and forcing the child to catch up on time missed. The curricular strands also address reading, arts & crafts, physical education, and activities of daily living.

The curricular strands focus on core academic skills related more directly to OT as well, such as fine motor skills, manuscript handwriting, and cursive handwriting. Handwriting encompasses pre-writing fine and visual motor skills as well as knowledge of manuscript and cursive letters. For these reasons, there are separate strands for each skill to more accurately assess and teach the students. There is also a strand solely for the legibility of handwriting because being able to accurately copy a letter does not mean that it is always legible. In some cases, students might rush, press to hard, or have difficulty staying on the lines. These students benefit from activities focusing on these skills rather than just arbitrary handwriting practice.

Section 2 has 3 strands and is designed for the middle and high school levels. This section focuses on relevant educational skills that are required for success in vocational tasks. The key for OT here is the skills that the students are completing. The strands do not addresses any one vocation over the other, but instead focus solely on skills that are required for most vocational pursuits.

Section 1

OT.1   Attention to Task While Seated: SI
    A. Postural alignment and control
    B. Body awareness
    C. Self regulation

OT.2   Attention to Task Seated: Behavior
    A. Self regulation
    B. Self awareness
    C. Reinforcement

OT.3   Pre-writing: Motor
    A. Hand separation
    B. Grasp patterns
    C. Shoulder girdle stability

OT.4   Pre-writing: Visual
    A. Line formation
    B. Shape recognition and imitation
    C. Left/Right awareness

OT.5   Upper Case Manuscript
    A. Directionality
    B. Letter size
    C. Object (Form) Perception
        1. Form constancy
        2. Visual closure
        3. Figure ground

OT.6   Lower Case Manuscript
    A. Directionality
    B. Letter height/differentiation
    C. Object (Form) Perception
        1. Form constancy
        2. Visual closure
        3. Figure ground

OT.7   Legibility of Handwriting
    A. Gradation of pressure
    B. Staying on lines
    C. Spatial perception
        1. Position in space: horizontal plane
        2. Position in space: vertical plane
        3. Depth perception

OT.8   Cursive Handwriting
    A. Motor planning
    B. Letter recognition
    C. Smoothness/quality of movement

OT.9   Reading
    A. Scanning
    B. Reversals
    C. Spelling

OT.10   Math
    A. Sense of quantity
    B. Math language
    C. Problem solving skills

OT.11   Arts and Crafts
    A. Bilateral integration and Crossing midline
    B. Hand Dexterity
    C. Scissor skills
    D. Tactile and Sensory Skills

OT.12   Physical Education
    A. Hand-eye coordination
    B. Gross motor skills
    C. Balance

OT.13   Activities of Daily Living
    A. Dressing
    B. Fasteners
    C. Feeding

D. Shoe Tying
E. Organizing Self
F. Organizing Environment

Section 2

OT.14   Technological and Academic Skills Affecting Vocation
     A. Note Taking
     B. Adaptive Equipment
     C. Typing/Keyboarding

OT.15.   Universal Vocational Skills
     A. Following Directions
     B. Generalizing Skills
     C. Compensatory Strategies

OT.16.   Energy Conservation and Body Mechanics
     A. Energy Conservation
     B. Proper Lifting Techniques
     C. Proper Reaching Techniques
     D. Proper Carrying and Transporting Techniques

Section 1

STANDARD OT.1
ATTENTION TO TASK WHILE SEATED - SENSORY
ALL STUDENTS WILL DEVELOP INCREASED POSTURAL, SENSORY, AND BODY CONTROL TO FACILITATE THE ABILITY TO MAINTAIN ATTENTION TO THE TEACHER, TASK, OR LESSON DURING ACADEMIC INSTRUCTION.

Descriptive Statement: The ability to focus on a task or lesson is paramount to the child to learn a new skill, concept, or idea. The time eschewed from the teacher to redirect the student is also mismanaged time that detracts from the classroom environment. This standard addresses the basic core requirement of paying attention to the teacher so that the student can actively engage in the learning process using a sensory integration model as the primary instructional tool.

Cumulative Progress Indicators

By the end of Kindergarten, students will:
A.   Postural Alignment and Control
  1. Sit with proper posture for 30 minute intervals without cuing.
  2. Be able to sit with feet on floor, shoulders back, and head up.
B.   Body Awareness
  1. Have fully integrated forward, backward, and sideways righting reactions.
  2. Have fully integrated Moro and Asymmetrical Tonic Neck Reflex(ATNR) reflexes.
  3. Be able to maintain balance in chair for entire school day without falling out or tipping chair over.
C.   Self Regulation
  1. Be able to identify 10 major body parts.
  2. Be able to walk on tiptoes.

3. Be able to tolerate varying textures such as soft, rough ,or hard.

Building upon knowledge and skills gained in preceding grades, by the end of 3rd Grade, students will:

A.   Postural Alignment and Control

1. Sit independently during teacher instruction to actively engage in the classroom lesson.

2. Maintain proper posture and body mechanics throughout the school day to decrease fatigue and slouching.

B.   Body Awareness

1. Be able to self correct posture in any situation whether it be static or dynamic for the purposes of maintaining active engagement in the lesson.

C.   Self Regulation

1. Maintain appropriate reaction to all environmental stimuli typically found during the school-year such as bells, fire alarms, and announcements.

2. Maintain appropriate self regulation during the academic day.

STANDARD OT.2
ATTENTION TO TASK WHILE SEATED - BEHAVIOR
ALL STUDENTS WILL DEVELOP INCREASED SELF REGULATION, SELF AWARENESS, AND REINFORCEMENT TO FACILITATE THE ABILITY TO MAINTAIN ATTENTION TO THE TEACHER, TASK, OR INSTRUCTION DURING ACADEMIC INSTRUCTION.

Descriptive Statement: The ability to focus on a task or lesson is paramount to the child to learn a new skill, concept, or idea. The time eschewed from the teacher to redirect the student is also mismanaged time that detracts from the classroom environment. This standard addresses the basic core requirement of paying attention to the teacher so that the student can actively engage in the learning process using a behavioral intervention model as the primary tool. These standards are generalized as specific behavior intervention plans (BIP) are typically developed by the child study team with or without an Applied Behavior Analyst (ABA) certified teacher or professional.

Cumulative Progress Indicators

By the end of Kindergarten and 3rd Grade, students will:

A.   Self Regulation
  1. Maintain appropriate reaction to the environment when presented with adverse stimuli.
  2. Maintain appropriate reaction to classmates and instructors.
  3. Develop strategies to self correct behavior to maintain appropriate self regulation.

B.   Self Awareness
  1. Be able to recognize when they are not acting appropriately in a physical sense.

2. Be able to recognize when they are not acting appropriately in an auditory/vocal sense.

3. Be able to recognize their own emotions and express those emotions appropriately.

C. Reinforcement

1. React appropriately to positive reinforcement to strengthen behaviors.

2. Demonstrate decreased need for reinforcement as good behaviors increase.

3. Demonstrate ability to express what reward/activity would be the most valuable to them.

STANDARD OT.3
PRE-WRITING SKILLS - MOTOR

ALL STUDENTS WILL DEVELOP THE PRE-WRITING SKILLS IN ORDER TO COMPLETE UPPER CASE AND LOWER CASE MANUSCRIPT LETTERS FOR THE PURPOSE OF WRITING, COPYING, AND RECOGNIZING THE 26 LETTERS OF THE ALPHABET.

Descriptive Statement: Pre-writing skills are the building blocks for all future handwriting and fine motor activities involving a tool or utensil such as paint brushes or string as well as pencils and writing instruments. This standard addresses the specific motor development of the hand and shoulder girdle that directly impact handwriting proficiency. This standard is also appropriate for beyond Kindergarten as most children do not have a consistent dynamic tripod grasp, hand separation, and intrinsic muscle strength until the ages of 6 or 7 years old and sometimes beyond.

Cumulative Progress Indicators

By the end of Kindergarten, students will:
A.   Hand Separation
> 1. Be able to utilize a three jaw chuck grasp with ring and pinky fingers pressed against ulnar side of hand independently.
> 2. Maintain ulnar side of hand on paper during fine motor and/or arts and crafts activities.
> 3. Complete in-hand manipulation skills activities to include translation, shifting, and rotation.

B.   Grasp Patterns
> 1. Be able to demonstrate the following gross grasp patterns independently to include: hook, power, spherical, and cylindrical.

2. Be able to demonstrate the following precision grasp patterns independently to include: lateral, tip, mature pincer, and key pinch.

C.   Shoulder Girdle Stability

1. Develop improved proximal skills mechanisms as evidenced by stabilizing the trunk in an upright position without the use of the arms.

2. Develop proximal stability to allow for increased distal (hand) control.

By the end of 3rd Grade, students will:

A.   Hand Separation

1. Demonstrate mastery of in-hand manipulation skills for functional school use to include rotating a pencil to erase paper.

2. Maintain ulnar side contact of hand while writing 100% of the time.

B.   Grasp Patterns

1. Maintain dynamic tripod grasp 100% of the time independently.

2. Utilize precision and gross grasp patterns independently for social studies and science labs.

C.   Shoulder Girdle Stability

1. Demonstrate mastery of patterns of mobility and stability utilizing the shoulder girdle and upper extremities to participate independently in academic activities.

STANDARD OT.4
PRE-WRITING SKILLS- VISUAL
ALL STUDENTS WILL DEVELOP THE PRE-WRITING SKILLS IN ORDER TO COMPLETE UPPER CASE AND LOWER CASE MANUSCRIPT LETTERS FOR THE PURPOSE OF WRITING, COPYING, AND RECOGNIZING THE 26 LETTERS OF THE ALPHABET.

Descriptive Statement: Pre-writing skills are the building blocks for all future handwriting and fine motor activities. This is especially true in that visual motor skills play a direct role in handwriting, arts and crafts, and academic subjects such as reading, language arts, and math. This standard addresses the building blocks of visual development that directly impact a student's academic performance. This standard is not appropriate beyond Kindergarten as more complex and detailed visual motor and visual perceptual concepts are addressed in other standards.

Cumulative Progress Indicators

By the end of Kindergarten, students will:

A.   Line Formation
1. Imitate vertical, horizontal, and diagonal lines without verbal cues and within 1/8" of the line provided.
2. Trace along irregular lines, paths, forms within a quarter of an inch.
3. Complete pictures with intersecting lines such as a standard cross or an "X".

B.   Shape Recognition and Imitation
1. Recognize the following shapes independently: circle, square, rectangle, and triangle.

2. Imitate the following shapes maintaining relatively the same size as the example: circle, square, rectangle, and triangle.

3. Connect a series of dots placed ½ inch apart to make simple drawings such as lines, circles, or squares.

C.   Directionality Concepts

1. Locate appropriate object when asked if object is on right or left.

2. Locate appropriate object when asked if object is up or down.

3. Locate appropriate object when asked if object is under or over.

4. Locate appropriate object when asked for similar concepts to the ones mentioned above.

By the end of 3rd Grade, students will be actively writing and should have mastered these skills before beginning a handwriting program.

STANDARD OT.5
UPPER CASE MANUSCRIPT

ALL STUDENTS WILL BE ABLE TO RECOGNIZE, COPY, AND IMITATE THE 26 LETTERS OF THE ALPHABET IN UPPER CASE MANUSCRIPT FORM UTILIZING A UNIFORM APPROACH FOCUSING ON DIRECTIONALITY, FORM PERCEPTION, AND SIZING.

Descriptive Statement: Manuscript letter writing is essential to academic success as it allows the student to utilize letters to form words to convey thoughts and ideas to instructors in all courses.

Cumulative Progress Indicators

By the end of Kindergarten, students will:

A.   Directionality

1. Start from the top and make downward lines to form letters to increase legibility.

2. Lift pencils when appropriate to properly form letters.

B.   Letter Size

1. Demonstrate understanding that all upper case manuscript letters are the same size.

2. Understand the importance of maintaining appropriate letter size for increased legibility.

C.   Object (Form) Perception

1. Demonstrate form constancy as evidenced by the ability to recognize forms and objects as the same in various positions, environments, and sizes.

2. Demonstrate visual closure skills as evidenced by the ability to name an object or form when part of the object is missing.

3. Demonstrate figure-ground skills as evidenced by being able to name foreground and background objects correctly.

By the end of 3rd Grade, students will:

A. Directionality
1. Start all letters from the top, making downward lines 100% of the time independently.
2. Appropriately form all upper case manuscript letters

B. Letter Size
1. Maintaining appropriate upper case manuscript letter size 100% of the time independently.

C. Object (Form) Perception
1. Demonstrate age appropriate form constancy as noted by recognizing a letter when it is typed, written in manuscript, cursive, italics, or bold.
2. Demonstrate age appropriate visual closure skills as noted by being able to locate partially covered items on your desk.
3. Demonstrate age appropriate figure-ground skills as noted by being able to visually attend to what is important.

STANDARD OT.6
LOWER CASE MANUSCRIPT

ALL STUDENTS WILL BE ABLE TO RECOGNIZE, COPY, AND IMITATE THE 26 LETTERS OF THE ALPHABET IN LOWER CASE MANUSCRIPT FORM UTILIZING A UNIFORM APPROACH FOCUSING ON DIRECTIONALITY, FORM PERCEPTION, AND SIZING.

Descriptive Statement: Manuscript letter writing is essential to academic success as it allows the student to utilize letters to form words to convey thoughts and ideas to instructors in all courses.

Cumulative Progress Indicators
By the end of Kindergarten, students will:

A. Directionality
    1. Start from the top and make downward lines to form letters to increase legibility.
    2. Lift pencils when appropriate to properly form letters.

B. Letter Size
    1. Demonstrate understanding that lower case manuscript letters are different heights and sizes.
    2. Understand the importance of maintaining appropriate letter size for each letter for increased legibility.

C. Object (Form) Perception
    1. Demonstrate form constancy as evidenced by the ability to recognize forms and objects as the same in various positions, environments, and sizes.
    2. Demonstrate visual closure skills as evidenced by the ability to name an object or form when part of the object or form is missing.

3. Demonstrate figure-ground skills as evidenced by being able to name foreground and background objects correctly.

By the end of 3rd Grade, students will:

A. Directionality

> 1. Start all letters from the top, making downward lines 100% of the time, independently.
> 2. Appropriately form all lower case letters.

B. Letter Size

> 1. Maintaining appropriate lower case manuscript letter size 100% of the time independently.

C. Object (Form) Perception

> 1. Demonstrate age appropriate form constancy as noted by recognizing a letter when it is typed, written in manuscript, cursive, italics, or bold.
> 2. Demonstrate age appropriate visual closure skills as noted by being able to locate partially covered items.
> 3. Demonstrate age appropriate figure-ground skills as noted by being able to visually attend to what is important.

STANDARD OT.7
LEGIBILITY OF HANDWRITING

ALL STUDENTS WILL UNDERSTAND AND DEMONSTRATE THE IMPORTANCE OF LEGIBLE HANDWRITING FOR THE PURPOSE OF EFFECTIVELY COMMUNICATING THOUGHTS AND IDEAS IN THE ACADEMIC SETTING.

Descriptive Statement: Legibility affects the student's ability to convey the correct thoughts, ideas, and answers. It is imperative for a student to fully express his or her thoughts so that they can be evaluated on merit, not on handwriting, omitted information, or other problems that occur when an evaluator cannot read your handwriting.

Cumulative Progress Indicators

By the end of Kindergarten, the student will:

A. Gradation of Pressure
    1. Recognize the differences in writing appearance due to increased or decreased pencil pressure.
    2. Develop intrinsic hand muscle strength to develop wrist and hand disassociation to decrease handwriting pressure.

B. Staying on Lines
    1. Maintain letters on the lines when writing upper case manuscript letters with 50% accuracy.
    2. Be able to make distinct corners for simple shapes such as a square or rectangle.

C. Spatial Perception
    1. Begin to recognize the relationship of figures and objects to oneself or other forms and objects.
    2. Begin to recognize the differentiation of letters and letter sequences in a word or sentence.

3. Begin to determine the relative distance between objects, words, and other forms.

By the end of 3rd Grade, the student will:

A. Gradation of Pressure
   1. Maintain appropriate pencil pressure to increase neatness.
   2. Maintain appropriate hand strength level for school based tasks including art and science labs.

B. Staying on Lines
   1. Maintain letters on the lines when writing all letters and words 100% of the time.
   2. Accurately imitate graphs and charts for science and math labs.

C. Spatial Perception
   1. Utilize appropriate spacing between letters in words, words between words, and maintain answers in allotted spaces for fill-in the blanks.
   2. Accurately maintain differentiated letter heights and letters that extend below the lines 100% of the time.
   3. Demonstrate appropriate depth perception for all classroom tasks including handwriting.

STANDARD OT.8
CURSIVE HANDWRITING
ALL STUDENTS WILL BE INTRODUCED TO THE MECHANICS, RECOGNITION, AND REPETITION REQUIRED TO ACCURATELY PRODUCE MANUSCRIPT IN CURSIVE FORM.

Descriptive Statement: Cursive handwriting is a very important life skill that can be challenging for some students due to the additional motor planning, visual memory, and increased quality of movement that it requires. This standard addresses the underlying skills needed for the student to succeed in cursive handwriting.

Cumulative Progress Indicators

By the end of Kindergarten, the student will:
A.   Motor Planning
   1. Begin demonstrating the ability to sequence motor actions forming a plan prior to carrying out the task.
   2. Begin demonstrating the ability to self correct through trial and error to create a motor plan.

B. Letter Recognition for cursive handwriting is not appropriate for this age level.

C.   Smoothness/Quality of Movement
   1. Begin to model slow and fast movements with a rhythmic timing with bilateral upper extremities.
   2. Begin to model slow and fast movements with a rhythmic timing with bilateral lower extremities.

By the end of 3rd Grade, the student will:
A.   Motor Planning
   1. Accurately perform the sequence of motor skills required to execute cursive handwriting.

2. Perform motor self correction in regards to formation of cursive letters 100% of the time.

B.   Letter Recognition

1. Accurately recognize all 26 letters of the cursive alphabet in lower and upper case forms with 100% accuracy.

2. Be able to switch independently from manuscript to cursive during reading and writing activities with 100% accuracy.

C.   Smoothness/Quality of Movement

1. Demonstrate a consistent rhythm when writing cursively to increase legibility.

2. Maintain pencil on paper for as long as possible when writing cursive words and sentences to increase writing quality.

STANDARD OT.9
READING
ALL STUDENTS WILL DEVELOP THE BASIC VISUAL MOTOR INTEGRATION SKILLS TO EFFECTIVELY READ WRITTEN TEXT IN BOOK FORM OR ON THE COMPUTER TO GAIN ACADEMIC KNOWLEDGE.

Descriptive Statement: Reading is a multi-faceted task that requires intact visual motor skills to accurately ascertain and interpret the information being presented. This standard addresses the specificity of these skills as it pertains to reading in the academic environment.

Cumulative Progress Indicators

By the end of Kindergarten, the student will:

A.   Scanning (Saccadic Eye Movements)

    1. Begin to develop the ability to accurately change fixation points rapidly in visual field from one stimulus to another.

    2. Begin to scan from the left to right and top to bottom for reading words and sentences.

B.   Reversals

    1. Demonstrate adequate visual discrimination skills to recognize symbols and words.

    2. Demonstrate adequate visual memory to master the alphabet and numbers.

C.   Spelling

    1. Begin to process simultaneous stimuli to accurately spell words.

    2. Begin to develop visual sequential memory since that is necessary for remembering the sequence of the letters in a word.

By the end of 3rd Grade, the student will:

A.   Scanning (Saccadic Eye Movements)

1. Be proficient with voluntary saccadic eye movements to accurately change fixation points in a visual field. For example, reviewing a paragraph and jumping from one line to the next to find information.

2. Become aware that figures and objects have a right and a left and apply this concept of laterality to proper scanning during reading activities.

B.   Reversals

1. Accurately recognize all letters 100% of the time without errors.

2. Utilize compensatory strategies for problem letter sets such as "b,d" or "p,q" if necessary.

C.   Spelling

1. Increase proficiency of visual sequential memory to increase vocabulary and spelling.

2. Increase visual-cognitive skills using sensorimotor cues such as clapping or music to increase spelling.

3. Utilize compensatory strategies to increase spelling such as a dictionary.

STANDARD OT.10
MATH

ALL STUDENTS WILL DEVELOP THE SPATIAL ORGANIZATIONAL SKILLS TO EFFECTIVELY COMPLETE MATHEMATICAL PROBLEMS TO INCLUDE BUT NOT LIMITED TO GRAPHING, CHARTING, COMPLEX ADDITION/SUBTRACTION, AND PROBLEM SOLVING SKILLS.

Descriptive Statement: Math is a very important subject that requires strong skill sets for organizing, sequencing, and interpreting data. Strong visual-cognitive skills compose the basic skill sets needed for higher level learning and academic instruction in mathematics. This standard addresses these basic visual-cognitive components.

Cumulative Progress Indicators

By the end of Kindergarten, the student will:
A.   Sense of Quantity
1. Identify which group out of 2 possible choices has a larger quantity without the need for mathematical computation.
2. Demonstrate emerging non-symbolic numerical skills through modeling, imitation, and repetition.
B.   Math Language
1. Demonstrate emerging generalizations for the concepts of numerals and quantity.
2. Correlate and name quantities using numerals.
C.   Problem Solving Skills
1. Be exposed to critical thinking and decision making through teacher modeling.
2. Be exposed to cause and effect concepts that are true in all mathematics.

By the end of 3rd Grade, the student will:

A. Sense of Quantity

   1. Be able to accurately identify quantities utilizing non-symbolic and symbolic numeral skills.

   2. Be able to correlate quantities in varying expressive mediums, i.e. charts, graphs, number lines

B. Math Language

   1. Be proficient in using basic math terminology such as addition, subtraction, multiplication, and division.

   2. Be able to utilize visual memory to recall math symbols and their meanings.

C. Problem Solving Skills

   1. Actively participate and demonstrate basic problem solving and critical thinking skills by breaking down task sequence, recognizing patterns, or eliminating the incorrect answer.

   2. Apply principles of cause and effect to mathematical ideas, theories, and equations.

STANDARD OT.11
ARTS AND CRAFTS
ALL STUDENTS WILL DEMONSTRATE BASIC FINE MOTOR AND TACTILE (SENSORY) SKILLS TO ACTIVELY PARTICIPATE IN ARTS AND CRAFTS ACTIVITIES DURING CLASSROOM AND INDIVIDUALIZED INSTRUCTION.

Descriptive Statement: Arts and crafts are valuable ways to explore your surroundings and begin to gain an understanding of yourself and the world around you. This standard focuses on fine motor skills and tactile (sensory) skills that directly affect the student's ability to participate in arts and crafts activities during the academic day.

Cumulative Progress Indicators

By the end of Kindergarten, the student will:

A.   Bilateral Integration and Crossing Midline
1. Demonstrate consistent hand dominance for all activities.
2. Reach across body for a given object utilizing dominant hand.

B.   Hand Dexterity
1. Demonstrate emerging in-hand manipulation skills.
2. Demonstrate emerging thenar and hypothenar eminences.

C.   Scissor Skills
1. Maintain appropriate grip for utilizing scissors focusing on wrist in neutral, thumb in primary hole, and pointer finger and possibly middle finger in secondary hole for stability.
2. Maintain appropriate motor action of lifting thumb up and down to cut.
3. Utilize non-dominant hand to stabilize paper.

By the end of 3rd Grade, the student will:

A.   Bilateral Integration and Crossing Midline
   1. Complete age appropriate two-handed tasks independently.
   2. Reach in all planes with dominant hand for object retrieval.
   3. Maintain stabilization of non-dominant side to allow for increased spatial exploration with dominant hand.

B.   Hand Dexterity
   1. Complete in-hand manipulation skills independently such as flipping over pencil to erase (rotation).
   2. Complete molding and cupping activities for applications in clay or mud utilizing both sides and eminences of hands.

C.   Scissor Skills
   1. Be able to cut out complex shapes and lines within 1/8" on the line without deviating.
   2. Be able to grade size and power of cutting stroke for finer and more detailed projects.

STANDARD OT.12
PHYSICAL EDUCATION

ALL STUDENTS WILL BE ABLE TO PERFORM BASIC MOTOR SKILLS TO ALLOW THEM TO PARTICIPATE IN HIGHER LEVEL PHYSICAL FITNESS ACTIVITIES REQUIRED IN PHYSICAL EDUCATION CLASS.

Descriptive Statement: All sports and games can be modified and broken down into the specific motor activities and skills that would increase success in physical education class. This standard addresses these universal coordination components that can increase the level of participation for all students.

Cumulative Progress Indicators

By the end of Kindergarten, the student will:

A.   Hand-eye Coordination
   1. Hit a target 12 feet away by throwing with an overhand motion using a tennis ball to hit a 2 foot target, 2 out of 3 trials.
   2. Catch a tennis ball from 5 feet thrown underhand in 2 out of 3 trials.

B.   Gross Motor Skills
   1. Complete varying hopping activities to include front, back, sideways, and hopping on 1 foot.
   2. Complete varying locomotion activities to include galloping, skipping, and running.

C.   Balance
   1. Walk on tiptoes in a straight line for 8 feet without heels touching the floor.
   2. Walk up and down stairs independently using a hand railing if required.

By the end of 3rd Grade, the student will:

A.   Hand-eye Coordination

1. Dribble a tennis ball with one hand for 10 consecutive times without error 1 out of 3 trials.

2. Dribble a tennis ball with alternating hands for 10 consecutive times without error 1 out of 3 trials.

B.   Gross Motor Skills

1. Complete 10 knee push-ups demonstrating core strength to maintain straight back and demonstrating upper extremity strength as evidenced by lowering of chest using elbow flexion and extension.

2. Complete 10 sit-ups demonstrating abdominal strength.

C.   Balance

1. Stand heel to toe on a balance beam with hands on hips for 10 seconds without falling off.

2. Stand on one leg on a line with eyes closed without falling or overly swaying for 10 seconds each leg.

STANDARD OT.13
ACTIVITIES OF DAILY LIVING

ALL STUDENTS WILL BE ABLE TO PERFORM ACTIVITIES OF DAILY LIVING (ADL) THROUGH LEARNING THE CORRECT MOTOR PATTERN, COMPENSATORY STRATEGIES OR ADAPTIVE EQUIPMENT AS NEEDED.

Descriptive Statement: All students need to be prepared to learn once in the classroom. This standard addresses the basic components of preparing oneself for school by being able to handle such activities such as dressing, shoe tying, and organizing so that they can focus on learning.

Cumulative Progress Indicators

By the end of Kindergarten, the student will:

A. Dressing
    1. Don/doff t-shirts, jackets, and button down shirts independently.
    2. Don/doff pants, socks, and shoes independently.
    3. Pull pants up/down for using the bathroom.

B. Fasteners
    1. Zip/unzip standard zipper for various articles of clothing.
    2. Undo/do snap fasteners for various articles of clothing.
    3. Undo/do Velcro fasteners for various articles of clothing.
    4. Undo/do large and medium sized buttons for various articles of clothing.
    5. Start a zipper by interlocking both ends using both hands.

C. Feeding
1. Utilize appropriate utensils for simple meals.
2. Open appropriate containers for foods and drinks.

D. Shoe Tying
1. Be able to untie single and double knotted shoes independently.
2. Be able to tie single and double knotted shoes independently.

By the end of 3rd Grade, the student will:

E. Organize Self
1. Independently sort school materials by subject and place in appropriate folder.
2. Be able to categorize like materials, instruments, or devices.
3. Have the ability to schedule tasks by priority order for homework, studying, or test taking.

F. Organize Environment
1. Demonstrate appropriate topographical organization skills to include instructions for execution of travel planes, recognizing places, keeping track of where one is while moving about, and anticipating features.
2. Maintaining a clean and clear workspace to increase productivity.
3. Maintain appropriate ergonomics/posture to properly relate to environment.

Section 2

STANDARD OT.14
TECHNOLOGICAL AND ACADEMIC SKILLS AFFECTING VOCATION
ALL STUDENTS WILL BE ABLE TO COMPLETE
TECHNOLOGICAL AND ACADEMIC TASKS
RELATED TO VOCATION

Descriptive Statement: The special needs high school student needs to be afforded the opportunity to be integrated into the community and have the opportunity for vocation post high school. This standard addresses the basic components of academic and technology uses to address vocation.

Cumulative Progress Indicators

By the end of 12th Grade, the student will:

A.   Note taking
   1. Utilize visual memory skills to increase speed and efficiency.
   2. Utilize abbreviations as appropriate to increase speed and efficiency.

B.   Adaptive Equipment
   1. Be given the necessary adaptive equipment to increase skill mastery and completion of tasks.
   2. Be able to recognize when adaptive equipment is needed for task mastery/completion and be able to notify supervisor.

C.   Typing/Keyboarding
   1. Utilize tactile skills to locate home keys for typing by feeling the bumps on the "F" and "J" keys.
   2. Accurately strike correct keys with correct fingers demonstrating hand dexterity skills.

STANDARD OT.15
UNIVERSAL VOCATIONAL SKILLS

ALL STUDENTS WILL BE ABLE TO COMPLETE UNIVERSAL VOCATIONAL SKILLS THAT CAN BE APPLIED TO MOST OCCUPATIONS.

Descriptive Statement: The special needs high school student needs to be afforded the opportunity to be integrated into the community and have the opportunity for vocation post high school. This standard addresses universal components of jobs that can be applied to many occupations.

Cumulative Progress Indicators

By the end of 12th Grade, the student will:

A.   Following Directions

1. Follow verbal directions with 100% accuracy utilizing short term memory skills, simplifying the instructions to single step directions, and/or making a task list.

2. Follow written instructions with the opportunity for instruction clarification if needed through the help of an aide or the use of a dictionary or thesaurus.

3. Utilize common sense and inferential skills to complete unspecified and/or commonly understood parts of a task that are not concretely explained.

B.   Generalizing of Skills

1. Apply specific skill to different job sites and/or trades. For example, using a tape measure is a specific skill that can be transferred to different trades.

2. Apply similar skill to different jobs or trades through the ability to generalize. For example, if there is not a tape measure available, demonstrate the ability to measure in an alternative way.

C.   Compensatory Strategies

1. Be afforded the opportunity to complete tasks with parts set up and/or modified to increase skill mastery.

2. Be able to recognize when a task requires modifications and be able to alert supervisor.

STANDARD OT.16
ENERGY CONSERVATION AND BODY MECHANICS
ALL STUDENTS WILL BE ABLE TO COMPLETE SIMPLE JOB RELATED TASKS SAFELY AND EFFICIENTLY REGARDLESS OF DISABILITY BY USING PROPER LIFTING TECHNIQUES AND ENERGY CONSERVATION PRINCIPLES.

Descriptive Statement: The special needs high school student needs to be afforded the opportunity to be integrated into the community and have the opportunity for vocation post high school. This standard addresses preventing injury and ensuring that once students earn vocational skills that they can maintain these skills safely.

Cumulative Progress Indicators

By the end of 12th Grade, the student will:
A.   Energy Conservation
>   1. Take appropriate breaks when working to conserve energy
>   2. Utilize appropriate tools and/or devices such as chairs or carts to conserve energy
>   3. Prepare work area prior to start of job with needed items and tasks readily accessible

B.   Proper Lifting Techniques
>   1. Maintain core principles of safe lifting during all aspects of job task
>   2. Be able to identify proper lifting techniques such as bending with your knees, maintaining a straight back, reducing the load, and squaring your body to what is being lifted

C.   Proper Reaching Techniques
>   1. Maintain nose to knees of principle that when items are higher than your nose a stool might be needed for safety and to bend your knees when items are below your knees

    2. If possible take a step closer to item being reached to reduce risk of falls or injury

D.   Proper Carrying and Transporting Techniques

    1. Maintain proper principles of carrying items close to body to reduce strain and decrease injury risk

    2. Maintain principle of pushing a cart when using a cart instead of pulling a cart to reduce risk of injury

Appendix A: Alternate Use Section

Coleman Curriculum for School Based Occupational Therapy is a valuable resource for the special education community. Hopefully, the curriculum can be utilized as intended in an integrative model, but this section is dedicated to everyone (therapists, parents, teachers, districts) who sees the value in a uniform model even though it has not been adopted by the entire team. The curriculum can be used as a focus guide for school based OT's, a training tool for teachers and as a teaching aid for parents who want to incorporate more skill development at home. All of these uses make the *Coleman Curriculum for School Based Occupational Therapy* a must have item for the continued development of academic motor skill task completion.

The curriculum can be used as a focus guide for OT's to adhere to appropriate school based objectives. It is very easy to continue to service students who demonstrate a need for outpatient or private occupational therapy, but no longer require school based OT. This curriculum strictly delineates the necessity for school based OT to focus on academic skill acquisition for increased academic success. Using therapy to increase coordination for athletics or to improve penmanship are two clear instances where the student has the necessary skills to complete appropriate academic needs, but the therapist or the district or the parent want further OT to increase the quality of the skill to a superior level. This increased refinement over the standard school level of academic necessity is a clear abuse and waste of taxpayer funded dollars. Skill acquisition for students is appropriate, skill refinement above what is necessary is waste. The therapist must be diligent to focus on these principles of skill attainment to exemplify the value of OT as a skilled service.

The teachers can also benefit from the curriculum as a training tool for them to increase their knowledge and understanding of age appropriate motor skill acquisition. Teachers are trained on learning and education principles, but not specifically on fine motor or visual motor development. Most teachers that I know explain that they use methods that have worked over the years or that were passed down from another teacher. The teachers who extrapolate the cumulative progress indicators and can cross reference them to their experiences find that they have a better understanding of the basis for all of these methods that worked for some reason. Now teachers have a tool to give them the reason. Teachers are also very motivated to learn more about how to help their students. This curriculum can be a springboard for them to read further in depth articles or books on anything from sensory integration to fine motor skill development. Knowledge and truth are as contagious as the common cold.

Finally, parents can utilize this text to increase their knowledge about their child's motor development and to gain a new perspective on the scope and intention of occupational therapy. Occupational therapy is intended to increase a student's skill set so that the student can learn at an appropriate pace alongside their peers. Students also mature and learn at different speeds. Most skills have a range to determine acceptable or typical motor development. For example, a mature pencil grasp develops between the ages of 5 and 7 years old. Some parents have been told that students should have a mature grasp in Kindergarten when in fact it is still developmentally appropriate to develop their grip for another one to two years. When parents can attain the understanding that development is a progression of one skill building on another skill to develop a finished product then they can eliminate their fear and focus on helping their child in the right way. For example, holding a pencil is not just the grasp. It is the culmination of the following predecessor skills: trunk stability, shoulder stability, hand-eye coordination, hand dexterity, separation of the sides of the hand, and distal stability. As most students can sit upright (trunk stability), we forget that this initial skill to interact with our environment is a necessary component to eventually lead us to hold our pencils correctly. Parents, teachers, and even therapists need to be reminded of these simple facts to properly train the students to complete the appropriate motor skill so that they can function independently in the academic environment.

Appendix B: Research Study

Effectiveness of a curriculum to deliver occupational therapy services in a school setting.

By Thomas Coleman, OTR/L

Abstract

This research paper focuses on a self-written curriculum, *Coleman Curriculum for School Based Occupational Therapy*, to address the inefficient and sometimes ineffective delivery of occupational therapy services in a school setting. The study focused on the therapist leading a 30 minute classroom group to address the student's motor, visual, and sensory needs. The study spanned 12 weeks focusing on Section 1 of the curriculum because it correlated to the age of the students. The curriculum is split into an elementary and a post elementary section. The lessons were planned to address each curricula strand at least one time to demonstrate to the students and teacher how effective occupational therapy can affect subjects such as math and reading. The curriculum aims to integrate educational relevance into school based occupational therapy. The results were as expected, but promising after the 12 lessons. Continued research is needed to further validate the utilization of a standard curriculum to increase student's motor skills, teacher carry-over into the classroom, and educationally relevant occupational therapy delivery of services.

Research Focus

My research focus was determining the effectiveness of utilizing an occupational therapy curriculum to deliver school based OT and its effects on student achievement (fine motor skills), teacher collaboration, and the educational role of occupational therapy in a school setting. I have already written a curriculum to address my concerns, but now I need to determine if it is valid and beneficial in a school setting. As an occupational therapist, I provide students with motor, visual, and sensory components to allow them to complete academic tasks closer to grade level so they can benefit from the lesson being taught by the educator. I try to align my activities with the educator, but in the current system teacher collaboration is not a primary focus in terms of training, materials, and time provided for therapist-teacher interaction. I hope to prove that a standardized curriculum can positively impact my three aforementioned concerns. I hope this study can encourage more study and exploration of making school based occupational therapy more in line with the least restrictive environment integrative model of education instead of relying on the current more medically based model.

For my research study, it will take place in 2 pre school classrooms where the children utilize the same educational curriculum. Class A will be the study group that receives the weekly OT lesson with the teacher being actively involved. Class B will be the control group receiving no instruction. I will provide 12, thirty minute lessons to Class A derived from my curriculum with written lesson plans just as a teacher does for their students during the school-year. I used autobiographical reflection, literature review, and teacher concerns to write my curriculum and determine my research focus. The curriculum that I wrote represents my beliefs that I have forged over my 11 years of providing school based therapy in multiple settings (public and private school) and in multiple states (NY and NJ). The current system does not match my personal beliefs of integration, transparency, and collaboration. This discrepancy, the continual pattern for the same teacher and student concerns in every place that I worked, and a reading self help books inspired me to write the curriculum. My professional ethics deem that I must fulfill my responsibilities of researching my vision before I publish it. I expect this curriculum to show some fine motor improvement, but even more teacher collaboration and educational relevance.

Literature Review

The research related to the positive effects of a school based occupational therapy curriculum supports my above theories and expected outcomes. The research literature addressed the importance of fine motor skills, student involvement, teacher involvement, and district concerns for the proposed new model of a curriculum. It also showed the concerns and frustrations with the old model of pull-out therapy. The research spanned from 1975 to the present as this was the year the USA passed the special education law, (the Education for All Handicapped Children Act, Public Law 94–142), which increased the amount of services provided to special needs children (Weintraub & Kovshi, 2004).The research also looked for other occupational therapy curriculums addressing student achievement. The only curriculums found were for teaching college level occupational therapy students.

Fine motor skills are very important in the academic life of pre-school and elementary school students as "30-60% of activities in each school day require the use of fine motor skills" (Chiu, Heidebrecht, Wehfmann, Sinclair, & Reid 2008, pg 30). Fine motor skills are important and affect self-help skills, social skills, and overall productiveness (Weintraub & Kovshi 2004). These studies help to corroborate the need and justification for school based occupational therapy.

Since there appears to be a definite need for school based occupational therapy in schools then it is necessary to administer this service in the most effective way possible. In educational settings, curriculum is the way a subject is taught. Curriculum serves two purposes; it gives the teacher and student a plan for learning and secondly, it gives everyone else a transparent and clear view of the intentions and expectations of the course. Spanish, Physical education, math, reading, and history all have curriculums, but not occupational therapy. This makes therapy isolated and ineffective. Mu & Royeen (2004, pg 244) stated,

"In an interdisciplinary model, service providers from different disciplines such as general and special educators, occupational therapists, physical therapists and speech and language pathologists work together in assessment and development of intervention programmes."

This article focuses on interdisciplinary effectiveness which is what an occupational therapy curriculum can promote. The educational setting requires collaboration to address student needs (Weintraub & Kovshi 2004).

The research points to the fact that collaborative models work and that fine motor skills are important in the everyday life of a student, but what did the research show about teacher involvement in occupational therapy? In one article, the researchers noted how the teachers had a limited knowledge of occupational therapy (Jackman & Stagniti, 2007). Their study went even further in relaying a quote from one of the teachers on page 171,

"I never knew that there was someone available to help out with [fine motor] activities to do in the classroom. I thought you just had to work activities out as best you could."

This clearly demonstrates that the current system is failing in collaboration with teachers. This lack of knowledge prevents some students from receiving a service that might benefit them (Jackman & Stagniti 2007).

One article that explored the restraints of the current school based occupational therapy systems and a route to inspire change was Critical reflections on school-based occupational therapy by Judy Beck Ericksen. This article explored the community, student, therapist, and teacher concerns with current school based therapy. The author took these concerns and chose a catalyst for change in a standardized test, the Assessment of Motor and Process Skills (AMPS. The author noted the positive change and increased collaboration among therapists as they increased uniformity in servicing the students. This gives me a lot of excitement as my catalyst for change is a curriculum, but I hope to influence and change similar things. The author stated this (pg 65) and it is exactly how I feel about my profession:

"I determined that we, as a group, needed to redefine and agree upon a common model for practice, a model that was based in occupation, and then to share this model with our constituent members."

Occupational therapist need to shift their intervention strategies due to the international shift from a medical based model to an educationally based model (Weintraub 2004). The curriculum , as a colleague of mine stated to me, is "revolutionary" in that it has never been done before to the best of mine or my colleague's knowledge. Weintraub and Kovshi state that 47 percent of a student's therapy time is spent outside of the classroom in isolation with just the therapist. They also state that most therapists are aware of how important it is to work with children in the classroom, but few have changed their practice patterns. Ironically, the study found that over 50% of teachers surveyed preferred that therapy be done outside the classroom. This is ironic but not unlike educational practices! The study states that therapy in the classroom disrupts learning according to teachers. I think this study shows the benefits of a curriculum. It would provide a tool to bridge the gap to increased teacher and therapist collaboration.

Purpose

The purpose of my research study is to determine if a curriculum can improve occupational therapy services to the student population through increased transparency, increased student skills, and increased teacher collaboration. The goal for the curriculum itself is to improve the quality, transparency, and effectiveness of school based OT which would help every member of the school district and community. The lesson plans and the teacher participating hands on are crucial as that is what an instructor would do. Currently, most students are taken out of class for therapy services so this study hopes to show how a standard curriculum can improve student skills, teacher knowledge, and transparency. The study has 1 primary research question and 2 secondary research questions. I was able to find a multitude of research on school based occupational therapy and the limitations of current models.

My primary research question is as follows: How effective will a school based occupational therapy curriculum be to increase student skills, specifically in terms of fine motor and visual motor skills? The primary focus of occupational therapy in school settings is to work on fine motor skills such as pencil grip, use of scissors, and fasteners for self care and visual motor skills specific to handwriting. Unfortunately, most parents and teachers are not aware of the component skills that lead to success in these tasks. The curriculum and research study will address these component skills and show educational relevance to promote increased independence in the classroom.

My initial secondary research question is as follows: In what ways will a school based curriculum increase teacher knowledge and student carry-over for fine motor skills? This how I plan to address teacher concerns that I have heard over the years and that I verified in my research study. In the current method of pulling students out of class to provide services, teachers are not privy to the details of that session. There is also no hands on experience or very little as collaboration with teachers is not scheduled in a normal day. The lesson plans I am providing during the study have a special collaboration section for the teacher to increase skill acquisition and carry-over.

My final secondary research question is as follows: In what ways will lesson plans affect the educational relevance of therapist directed activities? Currently, OTs write school modeled goals to assess skill acquisition and functional level, but they do not expand on any methodology to promote carryover in the classroom. In some IEP's, the therapist are relegated to the "motor" or "other needs sections". This displays the separation of the related services from the educational team because there is not a Core Curriculum Standard to reference like in academic subjects. Lesson plans correlated to a curriculum would encourage OT to focus and implement more functionally relevant educational activities which is the true purpose of school based OT. Therapy is one of the few areas in schools that does not have a curriculum and therefore does not require lesson plans.

Intervention

I conducted a 12 week study where I ran a 30 minute OT group in a Pre-K (4 yr. old) classroom using written lesson plans based on *Coleman Curriculum for School Based Occupational Therapy*. There are two classes. Class A, average age 59 months consisting of 12 students, was the study group that received the interventions and collaboration with the teacher. Class B, average age of 53.4 months with 9 students, is the control group that did not receive any intervention. Each class was tested before and after the 12 week study using the Beery Visual Motor Integration (VMI) test and sections of the Bruininks-Oseteretzsky Test of Motor Proficiency, second edition (BOT-2). The sections of the BOT-2 used were the short form, fine motor precision, fine motor control, and fine motor control. The VMI was administered in basic method A where there are 20 students or less and there are 2 adults present. The BOT-2 was administered in 2 ways. The fine motor sections were administered in class size group with the teacher aiding. The short form was administered in small groups of no more than 3 students with the therapist. Lesson plans and all materials provided before each lesson. The teacher was present and participated in each lesson to increase collaboration and carryover. The lesson plans also have a collaboration section where the OT specific skills and terms are explained thoroughly for the teachers. The teacher from Class A and the school's administration completed pre and post surveys describing their thoughts and impressions on the curriculum following the 12 week study. The teacher survey is important because it tries to address the shortcomings of the current pull-out OT service model and tries to increase collaboration and carry-over to increase student skill sets.

Setting

The school is a private Pre-K that offers infant to Kindergarten classes. It is located in Port Reading, NJ and is situated in a middle class neighborhood with urban towns bordering it very closely. This creates a mix in terms of race and socioeconomic status. The class has 12 students that are there Monday mornings at 9:30 am when the study was conducted. There are 13 students total in the class throughout the week, but there are only 12 present during the study. There are 5 boys and 7 girls in the class during lesson times. The teacher has over 3 years of experience at the school and is the head teacher. Besides the before care and aftercare, the school offers full day educational programs for all levels. The public school districts only offer half day programs for Kindergarten and do not offer Pre-K unless the child is special needs. This helps working parents and is one of the main reasons that this school has high enrollment. The private school structure was beneficial to my study because the teachers, administration, and parents can be more flexible and there are fewer hurdles to testing new programs. This a new curriculum and the school was very supportive and positive in this first research study on *Coleman Curriculum for School Based Occupational Therapy*. If it is successful then the school could utilize it and market it to increase class size. The private sector relies on new programs to get customers where as the public school does not need to solicit to get enrollment.

The goal of this study was to demonstrate the effectiveness of a standard OT curriculum to improve student performance, teacher performance, and educational relevance. The goal for the curriculum itself is to improve the quality, transparency, and effectiveness of school based OT which would help every member of the school district and community. The lesson plans and the teacher participating hands on are crucial as that is what an instructor would do. Currently, most students are taken out of class for therapy services so this study hopes to show how a standard curriculum can improve student skills, teacher knowledge, and transparency.

Data Collection

Primary: For the primary research question, the VMI and BOT-2 were administered pre- and post- study to determine changes in fine motor and visual motor skills. Specific skills such as pencil grasp and line directionality were noted as well as the standardized testing.

Secondary 1: For teacher knowledge I used inquiry data (surveys). Surveys showed the teachers opinion to see if they felt that their knowledge and skills were increased after the study. I also observed the hands on aspect of teacher participation and use a checklist to observe. The checklist allowed me to observe so that I can quantify how many lessons the teacher fully participated. I also used the checklist to determine if the teacher was prepared and then subsequently followed through during the week per teacher report. I am not there during the week to observe.

Secondary 2: For educational relevance I used observation data, specifically notes taken during the sessions. I also used artifacts as I am creating and implementing lesson plans, journaling, and personal narratives. The lesson plans directly showed an increase in educational relevance because all of the objectives are educationally based and correlate to a standard. A journal allowed me to express my feelings and observations as an OT trying to be an educator and adhering to an educational model.

Validity

The study is valid in many ways, but the strongest measure of validity is the transferability of the study. Any therapist can perform the lesson plans in a 4 year old Pre-K classroom and modify the lessons based on student level. Any teacher can participate regardless of experience. The study also has many applications because the curriculum standards are relevant from Pre-K to third grade. This comprises 6 levels of education that can be further tested using the standards and strands from the curriculum. Furthermore, the study is catalytic because further testing and exploration is encouraged. The validity is only limited by neutrality and democratic collaboration because I have designed and implemented the study independently. I researched and documented appropriately, but due to my strong beliefs I am emotionally and professionally vested in this study.

Results

The results demonstrated that *Coleman Curriculum for School Based Occupational Therapy* was a positive influence in Class A. The data proves this in terms of group and individual performance. In terms of group performance, the study group showed slightly higher increases in skills on standardized testing. In Table 1, Class A had an overall improvement in 4 out of the 5 tests. The differences are small, but are significant because of the short duration of the study. The study lasted 12 weeks instead of a full school-year which entails 40 weeks.

Test/Score	Pre-Standard	Pre-Scale	Post-Standard	Post-Scale	Difference
VMI	105.83		110.16		(+) 4.33
BOT-2 Short Form	46.50		49.75		(+) 3.25
BOT-2 Fine Motor Precision		10.25		11.41	(+) 1.16
BOT-2 Fine Motor Integration		15.25		13.83	(-) 1.42
BOT-2 Fine Motor Control	40.50		44.25		(+) 3.75

Table 1. Class A pre- and post study average class test scores

The results for Class B show that the control group remained the same, had a slight increase, or decrease in testing results. Class B did not have the consistently improved scores as the study group did. In Table 2, the VMI showed a change of 0.1 which essentially means that the control group did not show a change in skill level. This is in contrast to the study group that had a positive change of 4.33 in the VMI.

Test/Score	Pre-Standard	Pre-Scale	Post-Standard	Post-Scale	Difference
VMI	110.30		110.40		(+) 0.1
BOT-2 Short Form	48.14		50.00		(+) 1.85
BOT-2 Fine Motor Precision		10.85		9.71	(-) 1.14
BOT-2 Fine Motor Integration		14.50		14.00	(-) 0.5
BOT-2 Fine Motor Control	47.85		42.85		(-) 5.0

Table 2. Class B pre- and post study average class test scores

In terms of individual performances, Table 3 displays the three sections where students in Class A showed the most improvement. Student 8 displayed improvement in all three standardized tests rated by standard score. This student also demonstrated increased scores on the two tests measured with scaled scores making that student the only one to improve on all 5 tests. Student 11 showed the most improvement on the BOT-2 short form with a 15 point change in standard score. Student 5 demonstrated a 14 point increase in standard score for the VMI. This chart represents the improvement the students made following the 12 weeks of lessons focusing on educationally relevant OT skills and teacher carryover.

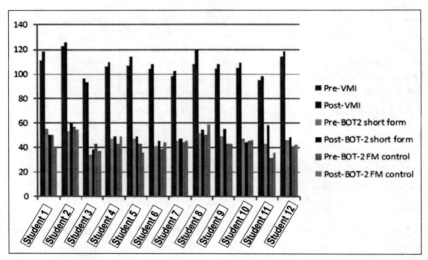

Table 3. Bar graph showing Class student improvements over course of study

The individual improvements are not measured solely on tests scores. Students increase skills on functional activities that do not show on tests. For example, Class A had many students attain a skill or improve upon a skill to improve their performance. The best example would be student 3. This student was unable to hop on 1 foot, held the pencil with a quadruped grasp with a thumb wrap, and could not draw a wavy line or a triangle in initial testing. He was able to hop on 1 foot, hold pencil against lateral side of thumb with verbal cues, and drew a triangle and curvy line on post testing. This student directly benefitted from the lessons as evidenced by the improved work samples and reports from the teacher. Student 10 was able to make a square during post-testing when this skill as not present during pre-study testing. Student 10 also maintains ulnar contact with the paper while writing with verbal cues from the teacher. Student 10 did not begin to do that consistently until after the lesson focusing on ulnar hand placement. The teacher was able to carry this skill over after the lesson.

This carryover demonstrated that teacher collaboration and knowledge base had been improved as well. The surveys further showed how much knowledge the teacher gained. In the pre-study survey regarding the impact of an OT curriculum, the teacher stated, "It will strengthen children's fine, gross, and visual skills." This is a very generic and broad statement. The post survey answers were much more specific and contained statements such as "The cue to pinch the pencil helped student 8 to hold the pencil so much better" and "I never realized how much shoulder strength affected handwriting". In my observations, the teacher seemed to enjoy participating in the lessons and gained knowledge through the process. The teacher was also critical in displaying the importance of skill components to the students. The positive and energetic presence of the teacher validated the use of OT to the students.

In terms of educational relevance, each lesson plan addressed an educational component specific to the age group. For example, in Lesson 5(Appendix B) the students read symbols from left to right because words and letters are symbols as well. The skill of scanning from right to left to read is independent of the specific symbol. The students drew geometrical shapes such as a circle and square and read them aloud instead of letters and words. In my journal, I noted how proud I was when the group ended because the students did very well and I think that it shows the educational relevance of using a curriculum. I don't know if that lesson occurs without a curricula strand addressing Reading. I am not sure what you mean by this statement.

Conclusion

The curriculum was effective in addressing fine motor, visual motor, and sensory motor skills in an educational setting. Standardized testing demonstrated a slight gain in the overall average of the study group. Individual scores and tasks achievements highlighted the act that some students benefitted more directly from the OT lessons. This can be attributed to appropriately designed lesson plans with an educational focus, teacher participation, and teacher carryover. The control group showed less gains on standardized testing and skill acquisition pertaining to test items. The study is limited by the size of the study, population of the study, and duration of the study. The merits of a standard OT curriculum to increase the effectiveness of school based occupational therapy shows promise. Further testing and research is encouraged to further validate and adopt this new way of thinking. During peer review, a colleague called *Coleman Curriculum for School Based Occupational Therapy* "revolutionary" in terms of its focus on integrating OT into education rather than viewing OT simply as a pull-out related service.

Appendix C: Lesson Plans from research study

Lesson Plan 1:
Pre-writing skills (visual and motor) for Pre-K 4 year old class

Objective: By the end of this lesson, students will have learned:

1. Imitate vertical line forming the line from the top to the bottom of the paper
2. Pincer grasp focusing on increasing web space
3. Separating sides of hand

Correlating Curriculum Standards (refer to Appendix A): OT.3, OT.4

Collaboration: By the end of the lesson, the teacher will have learned

1. Priming: completing a motor task or visual task that has the same components of the educational activity to increase competence and skill in the educational activity. In this lesson, tallying will prime line directionality as the students must make lines down to tally. Also, the block activity will be priming for pencil grasp.

2. Hand development: two sides of hand, one side for support and one side for precision, pincer grasp, web space..

Materials needed: Pencils, paper, and colored dice for the visual priming activity. 1 inch cubes, worksheets, and markers for the motor activity. The instructor will need to prepare the paper for the colored dice game with sections to tally green, red, and yellow. The instructor will need to bring in markers and worksheets for the motor activity.

Methods (Motor):

- The instructor will give each student at least 6 blocks or they can be shared and done in group.
- The students will stack the blocks into large towers with the instructor focusing on proper pincer grasp and maintenance of web space.
- Once the students have demonstrated a consistent grasp, dot to dot markers will be used due to their girth to carry-over grasp and web space. Worksheets will be used as deemed by instructor.
- Verbal cue for students to pick up markers can be, "Make letter C with your fingers like we practiced; pick up the marker, and flip it back in your hand so it rests in between your thumb and pointer finger (web space)."

Methods (Visual):

- The instructor will give each student a pencil and a sheet of paper with red, yellow, and green sections indicated for tallying.
- Dice with red, yellow, and green sides will be given to each group of students as one student will roll the dice and the others will tally. Each student will get a turn and each round can be repeated as necessary per instructor.
- The instructor will focus on students making vertical lines down from top to bottom.
- The instructor can also focus on students cupping their hands to roll the dice as this encourages hand development. (Thenar and hypothenar eminences demonstrated to teacher)
- Once the instructor feels the directionality is consistent, letter of the week can be practiced.

Assessment:

- By the end of the class period, every student should have had the opportunity to imitate vertical lines, demonstrate pincer grasp, and completed follow up activities for carry-over of skill.

Work for the week:

- Teacher should utilize priming strategies for hand development and/or directionality depending on needs of students.

Lesson Plan 2:
Pre-writing skills (hand development) for Pre-K 4 year old class

Objective: By the end of this lesson, students will have learned:

1. Motor plan appropriately to crawl, walk backwards, and hop from point A to B

2. Three jaw chuck grasp focusing on increasing maturity level of pencil grasp

3. Separating sides of hand

Correlating Curriculum Standards (refer to Appendix A): OT.3, OT.4, OT.8, OT.11

Collaboration: By the end of the lesson, the teacher will have learned

1. Motor planning: This is the ability to coordinate and sequence actions to complete a task that involves fine and/or gross motor movement. Crawling, hopping, and walking backwards require a specific motor sequence or plan to complete the task.

2. Three jaw chuck grasp: This grasp involves active participation of the thumb, pointer, and middle fingers while the ring and pinky fingers are pressed against the ulnar side of the hand. This correlates to the set-up of a dynamic tripod gasp which is the mature pencil rasp.

3. Hand development: two sides of hand, one side for support and one side for precision, pincer grasp, web space.

4. Spatial awareness: The ability to place objects in relation to another object which incorporates concepts such as left/right and up/down.

Materials needed: (2) Pre-drawn large construction papers with a snowman picture. Each snowman needs 3 circular sections, 1 arm on each side, and a top hat. Cotton balls, black pom-poms, multi-colored pom-poms, pennies, glue bottles, scissors, and a spot on the wall to hang the pictures

Activity: The students will glue cotton balls, pom-poms, and trees on the snowman picture. They will carry the object using a three jaw chuck grasp. They will assume this grasp by holding a penny under their ring and pinky fingers thus leaving their other fingers free to hold the manipulative.

Method:

- The instructor will divide the students into 2 groups. Each group will place the cotton balls, pom-poms, and trees on their specific picture.
- The classroom teacher will be at the first station helping the students to pick up the penny and make a three jaw chuck grasp.
- The therapist will be at the picture instructing the students on where to place the items.

    a. Cotton balls: top, middle, or bottom of snowman

    b. Black pom-poms: right or left arm

    c. Multi-colored pom-poms: hat or buttons

- There will be three rounds of coming to the picture to place items. Each round the students will come a different way (crawl, backwards walk, and hopping) and bring a different item (cotton ball, black pom-pom, or multi-colored pom-pom).
- Once the pictures are done on the walls, the students will sit at their desks and cut trees to place on the picture to finish it.

Assessment:

- By the end of the class period, every student should have had the opportunity to maneuver to the picture, take an item to the picture using a three jaw chuck grasp, cut out a tree, and glue the items in the appropriate spot after instructor's directions.
- The teacher will have had the opportunity to demonstrate and instruct each student on the three jaw chuck grasp.

Work for the week:

- Teacher should utilize three jaw chuck grasp in another activity to increase hand development which will lead to a mature pencil grasp for the educational setting.

Lesson Plan 3:
Pre-writing skills (manual dexterity) for Pre-K 4 year old class

Objective: By the end of this lesson, students will have learned:

1. Hand strength and dexterity to crumble tissue paper squares

2. Mature pincer grasp to hold and place tissue paper during activity

3. Bilateral integration skills to fold paper evenly

Correlating Curriculum Standards (refer to Appendix A): OT.3, OT.11

Collaboration: By the end of the lesson, the teacher will have learned

1. Hand strength: Some pencil grasps are compensation for decreased hand strength

2. Manual dexterity: This is the extent of skill one has using their hands to complete fine motor tasks

3. Mature pincer grasp: Being able to pick up an object using the pad of the pointer finger and the pad of the thumb

4. Bilateral integration: The ability to use both hands together to complete an activity or task

Materials: Construction paper, tissue paper squares, glue sticks or bottles, stickers, glitter, and crayons

Activity: The students will use tissue paper, markers or crayons, and decorations (stickers, glitter, etc.) to make a Valentine Day card.

Method:

- The instructor will have each student fold their piece of construction paper in half evenly.
- The instructor will draw a heart on the dry erase board and have each student copy it on the front of their card.
- The students will crumple tissue paper squares and glue them into the middle of the heart until the heart is filled.
- The students will open the card and write who the card is to and from after the teacher and instructor write the headings (to, from) for the students.
- The students will have time to decorate their card with crafts items (glitter, stickers, etc.)

Assessment:

- By the end of the class period, every student should have a completed card with each section finished.
- The teacher will have had the opportunity to demonstrate and instruct each student on the pincer grasp.

Work for the week:

- Teacher should utilize pincer grasp in another activity to increase hand development and manual dexterity

Lesson Plan 4:
Handwriting (multi-sensory) for Pre-K 4 year old class

Objective: By the end of this lesson, students will have learned:

1. Finger isolation (pointer finger)
2. Line directionality from the top to the bottom for the letters
3. Spatial relations when copying shapes
4. Tolerate varying textures during handwriting activity

Correlating Curriculum Standards (refer to Appendix A): OT.3, OT.4, OT.5, OT.6, OT.7

Collaboration: By the end of the lesson, the teacher will have learned

1. Finger Isolation: Ability to isolate 1 finger to complete a task

2. Directionality: How letters are formed from start to finish. The preferred method is from top down to the bottom as this increases legibility.

3. Spatial relations: The ability to relate one object to another based on position

4. Sensory processing: The ability of the student to tolerate or handle different inputs to their sensory system (touch, smell, sight, hearing, pressure/feel).

Materials: Shaving cream; dry erase board and markers for the teacher

Activity: The students will be seated at their desks with their desks cleared. The instructor will squirt shaving cream on their desk. The students will use both hands to smooth out the shaving cream and then use the pointer finger of their writing hand to make the letter of the week which for this lesson is "U" and "u".

Method:
- The instructor will have each student make an upper case "U" ensuring that they start from the top down. The students will practice the upper case "U" until satisfactory
- The instructor will have each student make a lower case "u" ensuring that they start from the top down. The students will practice the lower case "u" until satisfactory.
- The students will copy shapes after demonstrated by instructor (square, pentagon, and circle)
- The students will have free time to draw on their own and continue to experience the sensory input from the shaving cream.

Assessment:
- By the end of the class period, every student should have completed the letter of the week, the shapes, and had free time to draw with the shaving cream.
- The teacher will have had the opportunity to demonstrate and instruct each student on finger isolation, line directionality, and spatial relations for the shapes.

Work for the week:
- Teacher can use the shaving cream as a priming activity or introduction for a future letter.
- Continue to stress directionality and spatial relations to increase pre-writing skills.

Lesson Plan 5:
Reading for Pre-K 4 year old class

Objective: By the end of this lesson, students will have learned:
1. Scanning from left to write to simulate reading
2. Shape recognition
3. Spatial relations when copying shapes

Correlating Curriculum Standards (refer to Appendix A): OT.4, OT.9, OT.10, OT.11

Collaboration: By the end of the lesson, the teacher will have learned
1. Scanning: Ability to shift gaze from one object to another to locate an item
2. Skill attainment through component substitution: The ability to change components to work on the intended skill. For example in this lesson, the students read symbols other than letters to work on scanning from left to right when reading.
3. Spatial relations: The ability to relate one object to another based on position

Materials: Construction paper, sidewalk chalk, dry erase board and markers for the teacher

Activity: The students will be seated at their desks. The instructor will give each student a piece of construction paper and sidewalk chalk. The student will draw and color in the appropriate shape. The student will line up with their fellow students. They will hold the paper with the shapes facing the audience over their heads. One student will read the shapes from left to right.

Method:
- The instructor will assign each student 1 of 3 shapes in each round. So for round 1, the shapes will be circle, square, and triangle. For round 2, the shapes will be diamond, pentagon, and hexagon.
- After the students have made the shapes for that round, the instructor will split the students into two equal groups.
- The first group will bring their pictures to the front, line up, and hold the pictures up so everyone can see them.
- Each student from the second group will have the opportunity to read the symbols aloud just like reading letters and words. The instructor will tell the students holding up the symbols to switch spots for each student so they do not repeat the answer based on memory.
- The same procedure will be used for Round 2.

Assessment:
- By the end of the class period, every student should have completed 2 shapes, held their picture up for their peers to read it, and have the chance to read 2 times.
- The teacher will have had the opportunity to demonstrate and instruct these concepts.

Work for the week:
- Teacher can use skill attainment through component substitution for another reading lesson or in another subject area.
- Continue to incorporate multi-sensory activities into lesson plans

Lesson Plan 6:
Math for Pre-K 4 year old class

Objective: By the end of this lesson, students will have learned:

1. Sense of quantity

2. Cause and effect

3. Shoulder girdle strength

Correlating Curriculum Standards (refer to Appendix A): OT.1, OT.10, OT.12

Collaboration: By the end of the lesson, the teacher will have learned

1. Sense of quantity: Ability to determine larger quantity without mathematical equations

2. Cause and effect: The ability to see how one action will cause another action or event to take place

3. Shoulder girdle strength: The strength of the shoulders, back, and shoulder blade to maintain appropriate posture

Materials: 3 bins, a lot of something small like Legos™ that can be divided up, wooden shape blocks (cylinder and cube)

Activity: The students will place either a cylinder or a cube into one of three bins (empty, small quantity, large quantity) for 2 rounds. They will wheelbarrel walk for each round to get to the bins. They will complete a third round where they empty either the large or small quantity bin into the empty bin for cause and effect. They will army crawl (hands and elbows) for the third round.

Method:
- The students will line their chairs up two make a wide pathway on one end of the room. The bins will be placed on the other end of the room.
- The classroom teacher will hold the students legs so that they can wheelbarrel walk.
- The instructor will tell the students to pick an object (cylinder or cube) and place it in the appropriate bin (empty, small, or large quantity).
- Repeat the above for a second round.
- After round 2, the students will army crawl to the bins two at a time in side by side fashion.
- The instructor will ask them "What will happen if" questions prior to dumping and changing bin contents for cause and effect.

Assessment:
- By the end of the class period, every student should have completed 2 turns of math quantity and 1 round of cause and effect.
- The teacher will have had the opportunity to demonstrate and instruct these concepts.

Work for the week:
- Teacher can perform follow up lessons on sense of quantity and cause/effect to increase student carry-over.
- Continue to incorporate multi-sensory activities into lesson plans

Lesson Plan 7:
Attention to task using sensory integration strategies for Pre-K 4 year old class

Objective: By the end of this lesson, students will have learned:
1. Attention to task
2. Cause and effect
3. Positive reinforcement

Correlating Curriculum Standards (refer to Appendix A): OT.1, OT.3, OT.12

Collaboration: By the end of the lesson, the teacher will have learned

1. Self regulation: Ability to maintain appropriate behavior in terms of body movement, environmental interaction, and social interaction.

2. Cause and effect: The ability to see how one action will cause another action or event to take place

3. Sensory integration: The ability of the person to modulate the sensory input from the environment in terms of the body's 5 natural senses which are touch, taste, smell, sound, and sight. This also includes the role of the vestibular system and muscle tone in terms of need for movement and difficulty remaining still.

Materials: ample floor space, finger paint, cut up sponges, bowls for the paint, white paper, paper towels

Activity: The students will participate in 2 sensory motor activation activities prior to completing a tabletop visual motor integration activity. The sensory motor activities are for shoulder girdle stability and activation. Both sensory motor activities require partners. In the first activity, the students stand opposing each other and scissor their legs so that one leg is forward and one leg is back. The students then press their palms against the other students' palms and push against each other for a count of 10 seconds. In the second activity, one student attempts to hold their arms straight out in front of them at shoulder level. Their partner slowly pushes the other student's arms down to their sides for a count of 10 seconds. The tabletop visual motor activity requires the students to make the infinity sign or a sideways figure 8 with the students focusing on completing the pattern without lifting the sponge to encourage the student to cross midline and go in all four quadrants.

Method:

- The instructor and teacher will clear ample floor space for the 2 sensory motor activities.
- The instructor will call each pair of students to perform the first sensory motor activity. After each pair has gone, the instructor will call each pair of students again to perform the second sensory motor activity.
- The instructor will have the students sit at their seats. Each student will get a piece of paper and a small bowl with paint and a sponge cut into a 1.5" square piece.
- The students are to utilize a three jaw chuck grasp to grab and hold the sponge for the activity.
- The instructor will demonstrate the infinity sign and go from table to table to help each student.
- The teacher will also go from table to table to help the students.
- The students are to make the infinity sign without lifting their sponges and are encouraged to do it multiple times. The students can also switch bowls to make new colors once each student has made an acceptable infinity sign. The instructor and teacher can use this time to work on color formation and interaction as well.

Assessment:

- By the end of the class period, every student should have completed 2 rounds of sensory motor activities and 1 visual motor integration activity (infinity sign).
- The teacher will have had the opportunity to reinforce three jaw chuck grasp, observe sensory motor activities, and participate hands on for the visual motor activity.

Work for the week:

- Teacher can use the sensory activation activities or can seek to learn further activities from the therapist to perform prior to seat work to increase attention to task.
- Continue to incorporate grasp, sensory, and visual motor activities during the academic day to enhance and strengthen overall student skills.

Lesson Plan 8:
Attention to task using behavior strategies for Pre-K 4 year old class

Objective: By the end of this lesson, students will have learned:

1. Attention to task
2. Cause and effect
3. Positive reinforcement

Correlating Curriculum Standards (refer to Appendix A): OT.2, OT.3, OT.12

Collaboration: By the end of the lesson, the teacher will have learned

1. Self regulation: Ability to maintain appropriate behavior in terms of body movement, environmental interaction, and social interaction.
2. Cause and effect: The ability to see how one action will cause another action or event to take place
3. Positive reinforcement: Being awarded items or praise for appropriate behavior.

Materials: stamper, behavior chart with students names and columns for earning stamps for appropriate behavior, stickers as a reward, ample floor space

Activity: The students will participate in the game of Simon Says with the instructor leading. The teacher will help monitor behavior. The students can earn one stamp for winning the game, one for following directions for not talking, and one for following directions for staying seated when eliminated during each round. There will be a practice round and then 2 rounds for the game. Each student can earn up to 6 stamps.

The student needs to earn 4 stamps for the positive reinforce of stickers.

Method:
- The instructor and teacher will clear ample floor space for the game and designate a sitting area for eliminated players.
- The instructor will space the students appropriately so that each student has ample space to raise arms overhead and to the side.
- The instructor will lead the practice round then the first round of Simon Says.
- Once the round is over, the students will be called by name and walk to the behavior chart. They will utilize a three jaw chuck grasp to stamp in each column that they have earned.
- Repeat for Round 2.
- The instructor will give out stickers to the students who earn 4 or more stamps.

Assessment:
- By the end of the class period, every student should have completed 2 rounds of Simon Says.
- The teacher will have had the opportunity to observe how a behavior chart can monitor and possibly improve student behavior and attention to task.

Work for the week:
- Teacher can utilize a behavior chart if deemed necessary to increase student attention to task and behavior.
- Continue to observe and assess student attention to task to ensure that academic material presented is reaching the students.

Lesson Plan 9:
Activities of daily living for Pre-K 4 year old class

Objective: By the end of this lesson, students will have learned:
    1. Open and close fasteners (buttons, Velcro, buckles, zippers) for self care
    2. Introduced to loop, swoop, and pull method of tying shoes
    3. Lacing

Correlating Curriculum Standards (refer to Appendix A): OT.13

Collaboration: By the end of the lesson, the teacher will have learned
    1. Self care skills: Best grasp and hand position for ADL tasks involving fasteners
    2. Backward chaining: Completing a task step by step starting in reverse so that each time the student attempts the task, the student completes the task regardless of what step the student starts at.

Materials: lacing boards with string, wooden lacing shoe, fastener boards or fastener doll

Activity: The students will complete one lacing board using a single stitch pattern. The students will open and close the fasteners on the therapist chosen material. Each student will be introduced to shoe tying using the loop, swoop, pull method and utilizing backward chaining.

Method:
- The instructor will pass out lacing boards to each student.
- The instructor will demonstrate the stitch pattern. The

teacher and instructor will go from student to student to provide assistance as needed.

• When the students are done lacing, one half of the class will do fasteners and the other half will complete shoe tying. The students and professional will switch once the task is completed so that each party completes both tasks.

• The instructor will demonstrate backward chaining so that the teacher can complete it hands on with the students.

• The instructor will demonstrate proper gasp patterns and tips for completing fasteners. For example, to undo a button if you pinch the button with one hand and the fabric with the other you can pull them apart to find the hole to push the button through. Tips like these to add a visual component can make the activity easier for the student.

Assessment:

• By the end of the class period, every student should have completed 1 lacing board, completed all of the fasteners, and be introduced to shoe tying using backward chaining.

• The teacher will have had the opportunity to practice all tasks hands-on with students.

Work for the week:

• Teacher can use the self care skills to foster student independence in A.M. or P.M. routines.

• Practice shoe tying using backward chaining method.

Lesson Plan 10:
Ulnar hand placement for Pre-K 4 year old class

Objective: By the end of this lesson, students will have learned:
1. To keep their pinky side (ulnar) of their hand placed on paper when writing, coloring, or drawing
2. How to grade pressure when doing fine motor activities
3. Making and classification (odd or even) of numerals

Correlating Curriculum Standards (refer to Appendix A): OT.3, OT.4, OT.7, OT.9, OT.11

Collaboration: By the end of the lesson, the teacher will have learned
1. Ulnar (pinky side) hand placement: The pinky (ulnar) side of the hand provides the base of support for the thumb (medial) side of the hand to perform precise movements.
2. Gradation of pressure: The force applied while pressing against an object. So for handwriting, if you press too hard on the paper your letters are dark, but if you press too easy your letters are very faint.

Materials: black coated scratch paper, coins, tongue depressors, circular pad made from cloth or felt, etching stylus

Activity: The students will complete etching activity on etching paper. The instructor will prepare each paper with 1 line centered across to make 2 halves. The students will use a different tool in each half to etch a number from 1 to 12. Odd numbers will go on top and even numbers will go on the bottom. The students will draw 1 number from a bag and the class will draw the numeral on the proper half.

Method:

- The instructor will pass out etching paper, already prepared, to each student.
- The instructor will pass out tools to each student with the students attempting each tool (coin, etching stylus, tongue depressor) and a felt or cloth pad for ulnar hand placement
- Demonstrate using each tool and using the pad properly focusing on the student keeping the pinky (ulnar) side pressed on the pad.
- The instructor will call one student at a time to pick a number from the bag. After the number is drawn, each student will write the number in the appropriate area (top for odd, bottom for even). Continue until all the numbers are gone.
- After every four rounds, have students exchange writing instruments so that each student gets to try a different one.

Assessment:

- By the end of the class period, every student should have completed all 4 quadrants using a different tool for each.
- The teacher will have had the opportunity to practice all tasks hands-on with students.

Work for the week:

- Teacher will monitor gradation of pressure of students' handwriting to see if it needs to be addressed.
- Teacher will cue, prompt, and model as necessary ulnar hand placement to increase grasp development and overall handwriting

Lesson Plan 11:
Sequencing and motor planning for Pre-K 4 year old class

Objective: By the end of this lesson, students will have learned:
1. Sequencing items in the proper order
2. Motor planning
3. Following directions

Correlating Curriculum Standards (refer to Appendix A): OT.8, OT.12, OT.13, OT.15

Collaboration: By the end of the lesson, the teacher will have learned

1. Motor planning: This is the ability to coordinate and sequence actions to complete a task that involves fine and/or gross motor movement.

2. Sequencing: Placing items in the proper order. This helps increase organization.

Materials: ample floor space, Sandwich Stacking Game, chairs

Activity: The students will separate into 2 equal teams. In each round of the game, there will be one leader who calls out the next topping on the sandwich in the proper sequence. After each round, the students will change roles so that every student can be the leader and sequence the sandwich toppings. When a topping is called and the student has to bring it to the leader. The instructor will set a new motor movement to get to the leader. Some examples are walking backwards or sideways. The team that gets the most sandwiches made in the right order first wins.

Method:
- The instructor and teacher will set the room up with ample floor space and chairs for the students to sit.

- The instructor will separate the students into 2 equal teams.
- The instructor will demonstrate and explain the game.
- In the first round, the instructor will pick the leader and he/she will stand across the room from their teammates. The instructor will demonstrate and assign the motor activity for this round. The team that completes the sandwich first in the proper order while doing motor activity receives 1 point.
- In each round thereafter, the instructor will assign a new leader and a new motor activity.
- After all of the rounds have been completed, the scores will be tallied and the winner announced.

Assessment:
- By the end of the class period, every student should have been a leader once and tried all but one motor movement.
- The teacher will have had the opportunity to practice all tasks hands-on with students.

Work for the week:
- Teacher will use principles of sequencing to address student organizational difficulties as needed.

Lesson Plan 12:
ADL's (Tool use and following recipe) for Pre-K 4 year old class

Objective: By the end of this lesson, students will have learned:
1. Tool use to include manual apple corer and manual orange juicer
2. Following directions for recipe
3. Measuring amounts

Correlating Curriculum Standards (refer to Appendix A): OT.3, OT.10, OT.13

Collaboration: By the end of the lesson, the teacher will have learned
1. Tool use: It is important to expose students to the need for proficient tool use in school and home. It encompasses fine and gross motor skills. It also can help increase student mastery and increase self esteem.

Materials: Fresh fruit: apples, bananas, and oranges, Frozen fruit: strawberries, blueberries, raspberries, and blackberries.

Equipment: apple corer(the kind where you press down on the apple so it is sliced and cored), orange juicer (manual), knife, cutting board, cups, bowls, blender, electric juicer, measuring cups

Activity: The students will utilize manual and electric tools and appliances to make fresh fruit smoothies. They will follow directions for a recipe and measure the appropriate amounts of items. There will be 2 smoothie types made and each student will have the opportunity to participate in making both smoothies. The first smoothie will be orange juice, banana, and frozen strawberries and is called California Dreaming. The second smoothie will be apple juice and frozen blackberries, frozen raspberries, and frozen blueberries and is called Berry Blast.

Method:

- The instructor will divide the tools and ingredients for each smoothie. Each smoothie making process will entail making the juice, adding the ingredients, and blending.
- The instructor will separate the students into 2 groups so that each group gets to make one juice and add one set of ingredients. For example group A will make the orange juice and group B will add the fruit. For the next smoothie, they will be reversed. Group B will make the juice and Group A will add the fruit.
- The tools for California Dreaming required are cutting board, knife, manual orange juicer, measuring cups and blender.
- The tools for Berry Blast are apple corer, electric juicer, measuring cups, and blender.
- The recipe for California dreaming: 2 cups of orange juice, 1 banana, and 2-3 cups of frozen strawberries placed in a blender and blended until smooth.
- The recipe for Berry Blast: 2 cups apple juice, ½ cup blackberries, ½ cup raspberries, and 2-3 cups of blueberries placed in a blender and blended until smooth.

Assessment:

- By the end of the class period, every student should have had the opportunity to use a tool to juice the fruit and used a measuring cup to add the ingredients.
- The teacher will have had the opportunity to practice all tasks hands-on with students.

Work for the week:

- Teacher will recognize the importance of tool use and incorporate into teaching as needed.

Motor Skill Age Equivalents for Common Academic Tasks

3-4 years
- Draws circle
- Cuts paper into 2 pieces
- Laces 3 holes
- Draws a cross
- Grasps marker with thumb and pad of index finger, other 3 fingers are secure against palm, upper portion of marker rests between thumb and index finger, child moves hand as a unit when drawing.
- Buttons and unbuttons 1 button
- Walks up 4 steps without support placing 1 foot on each step
- Catches 8-inch ball with arms extended
- Runs and stops without falling
- Using overhand toss hits target from 5 feet
- Kicks a stationary ball using a 2-step start
- Cuts across paper following a curved line/circle
- Folds paper three times
- Draws a square following a model
- Unzips and unsnaps clothing
- Closes 2 of 3 front snaps
- Buttons front opening clothing
- Beginning of shift and complex rotation with easy to handle objects
- Stabilize paper for coloring/writing

4-5 years
- Draws a square independently
- Connects dots by drawing a straight line
- Grasps marker between thumb and pad of index finger, marker rests on first joint of middle finger
- Folds paper in half lengthwise with edges parallel
- Colors between vertical lines

- Bounces and catches a small ball
- Completes three sit-ups
- Catches a small ball with hands only from 5 feet away
- Using an overhead toss hits target from 12 feet
- Draws a triangle
- Traces own name
- Locates first, middle, and last in group of objects
- Remains on task for 5-10 minutes when distractions are present
- Draws diamond, imitating adult
- Names classes/categories of sorted objects
- Identifies and counts quantities of at least 6
- Gallops forward
- Completes picture of a stick person
- Cuts out small square/triangle with scissors
- Traces around own hand
- Dresses independently when asked
- Opens container and removes food
- Carries liquid in open container, without spilling
- Able to rotate marker into writing position regardless of prior position
- Stabilize paper for coloring/writing
- Begins creative play
- Distinguishes right and left on self
- Uses a mature lateral grasp of spoon or fork
- Uses a knife for spreading
- Identifies directionality concepts of on, under, behind, and beside in relation to body
- Uses preferred hand with increasing coordination

5-6 years
- Folds paper in half twice with edges parallel
- Using opposing arm and leg movements and initiating kick by extending leg back with bent knee, kicks ball so it travels 12 feet in the air

- Names capital and lower case letters when shown printed letters
- Matches (visually) identical letters in group of different letters
- Prints letters and numbers, copying a model
- Scans letters of word left to right
- Identifying missing or incongruent element of picture
- Improvises body movements to follow rhythm/tempo
- Prints own first name without a model
- Reads and writes numerals to 19
- Counts orally to 100
- Walks down stairs carrying an object
- Skips forward
- Lifts body off the floor to complete one push-up
- Cuts out pictures following general shape
- Cuts cloth/other material with scissors
- Makes fine visual discrimination, matches letters that look very similar
- Ties shoes, following step by step instruction
- Put laces in shoes and laces correctly
- Mature grasp for cutting develops
- Brushes teeth without supervision

6-7 years
- Completes 5 sit-ups
- Completes 8 push-ups
- Bounces and catches a small ball
- Folds paper in half lengthwise twice with edges parallel
- Reads and writes numerals to 49
- Writes lower case and upper case manuscript letters from memory with consistent letter formation
- Ties shoes without model
- Figure-ground perception stabilizes/begins to mature
- Dramatic improvement in form constancy
- In-hand manipulation skills become more consistent

- More complex cutting skills develop
- Does simple errands

8+ years
- Position in space development complete at 7 to 9 years of age
- Spatial relationships improves to approximately 10 years of age
- Refinement and mastery of manuscript handwriting
- Introduction and refinement of cursive handwriting
- Manages small amounts of money
- Uses telephone correctly
- Begins play for games/recreation
- In-hand manipulation skills defined

BIBLIOGRAPHY

Allen, A.S., Cas-Smith, J., & Pratt, P.N. (1996) *Occupational therapy for children, Third edition.* St.Louis, MO: Mosby-Year Book, Inc.

Barnes, M.R., &Crutchfield, C.A., & Heriza, C.B.(1978) *The neurophysiological basis of patient treatment, Volume 2 (Reflexes in motor development).* Atlanta, GA: Stokesville Publishing.

Bly, L. (1983) *The components of normal movement during the first year of life and abnormal motor development.* Chicago, IL: Neuro-Developmental Treatment association, Inc.

Cernak, S.A. & Tseng, M.H. The influence of ergonomic factors and perceptual-motor abilities on handwriting performance. The American Journal of Occupational Therapy 1993; volume 47; number 10; pp 919-926.

Chin, T., Heidebrecht, M., Wehrman, S., Sinclair, G., & Reid, D. (2008). Improving teacher awareness of fine motor problems and occupational therapy: Education workshops for preservice teachers, general education teachers and special education teachers in Canada. International Journal of Special Education, 23(3), 30-38.

Danielson, C. (1999) Components of professional practice. Educational testing service.

Dunn, W. (1999) *Sensory profile.* USA: The Psychological Corporation.

Furuno, *et al* & Parks, S. (1984-2004) Revised HELP Checklist birth to three years old: Palo Alto, CA: VORT Corporation.

Furuno, *et al* & Parks, S. (1984-2004) Revised HELP Checklist three years to six years old: Palo Alto, CA: VORT Corporation.

Hemmingson, H. & Penman, M. (2010). Making children's voices visible: The school setting interview. *Kairaranga*, 11(1), 45-49.

Jackman, M. & Stagnitti, K. (2007). Fine motor difficulties: The need for advocating for the role of occupational therapy in schools. *Australian Occupational Therapy Journal*, 54, 168-173.

Kulp, M.T. Relationship between visual motor integration skill and academic performance in kindergarten through third grade. Optometry and Vision Science 1999; vol. 76; no. 3; 159-162.

Miller, R. & Walker ,K.(1993) *Perspectives on theory for the practice of occupational therapy.* Gaithersburg, MD: Aspen Publishing.

Montgomery, P.C. & Richter, E.W (1988) *The sensorimotor performance analysis.* Hugo, MN: PDP press.

Mu, K. & Royen, C. (2004). Interprofessional vs. interdiscipliary services in school based occupational therapy practice. *Occupational Therapy International*, 11(4), 244-247.

Murray-Slutsky, C. & Paris, B. (2005) *Is it sensory or is it behavior.* San Antonio, TX: Harcourt Assessment.

New Jersey Core Curriculum Content Standards for Science used as a skeleton, pp 97-127.

O'Flynn, J. Improving math performance. Advance for Occupational Therapy 10-12-2009; 32-34.

Peabody Developmental Motor Scales, Second Edition: Austin, TX; Pro-Ed Inc. Kaplan, B.J., Law, M., Pollock, N., & Wilson, B.N. (1994) *Clinical observations of motor and postural skills (COMPS).* Framingham, MA: Therapro. Inc.

Reed, K. & Sanderson, S.N.(1992) Concepts of occupational therapy. Baltimore, MD: Williams &Wilkins.

Shellenberger, S. & Williams, M.S (1994). *How does your engine run?* Albuquerque, NM: TherapyWorks, Inc.

Terry, B. Overcoming learning roadblocks. http://www.bonnieterrylearning.com/learning-roadblocks/

Vreeland, E. (1998) *Handwriting: not just in the hands.*
Springfield, NH: Maxanna Learning Systems.

Weintraub, N. (2004). School based occupational therapy: An
internal perspective. Occupational Therapy International,
11(1), 3-5.

Weintraub, N. & Kovshi, M. (2004). Changing practice
patterns of school based occupational therapy in Israel.
Occupational Therapy International, 11(1), 40-51.

For more about the author

◆ E-mail tcoleman56@comcast.net

◆ Reaching Higher Therapy website
www.reachinghighertherapy.com

◆ Personal Facebook page
https://www.facebook.com/thomas.coleman.942

◆ Reaching Higher Therapy Facebook page
https://www.facebook.com/pages/
Reaching-Higher-Therapy/234565483228641

◆ Follow me on Twitter under @OTwithaplan

◆ Join me on LinkedIn! under my name, Thomas Coleman.

Warnock Pro on LSI 50# white
Type and Design by Karen P. Stone

ENDORSEMENTS

Comprehensive and revolutionary, *The Coleman Curriculum for School Based Occupational Therapy* provides innovative insight into an educational program that streamlines occupational therapy in the classroom for therapists, educators, students, and parents; in an effective and systematic manner that gives transparency to occupational therapy techniques. Issues that arise from current occupational therapy practices in the education system is remodeled with a tiered system of learned skills and lesson plans that guarantee a synergistic change in the educational experience for special needs students amongst their peers and alleviates the stress caused by the current model to teachers and parents.

Coleman presents a curriculum that focuses on putting the student first, while having teachers and parents cultivate a better learning environment that will give students the necessary skills to continuously thrive in their education, and put enjoyment back into learning for everyone.

Fawn B. Stephens, Psychology Graduate of Rutgers University

Coleman's use of curricular strands and lesson plans show how OT can be better integrated in the schools for all children. This curriculum can be an asset for therapists and teachers alike.

Dr. Richard Flamini, Director Denville Board of Education

I loved this book! I think it will help me as I explain OT to parents and teachers so that they can see how I help their children.

Tara Lichter, School Based Occupational Therapist

Coleman takes a revolutionary take on school based therapy in this exciting new book where he promotes educational ideas such as curriculum and lesson plans over standard OT goals and pull-out treatment.

Shana Fawkes, School Based Occupational Therapist

CPSIA information can be obtained at www.ICGtesting.com
Printed in the USA
BVOW02s1915180314

348045BV00005B/6/P